Nine Roads to Wealth

DAVID L. MARKSTEIN

McGRAW-HILL BOOK COMPANY
New York   St. Louis   San Francisco   Dusseldorf   London
Mexico   Panama   Sydney   Toronto

NINE ROADS TO WEALTH

To Donald, Genevieve, Anne, and Robert

Preface

"GOOD-BYE MILLIONAIRES. There won't be any new ones because high income taxes make it impossible." So said the
gloomy economic prophets when, after World War II, it became apparent that high taxes were a permanent fixture and
that high incomes would be siphoned off to the Treasury during all the foreseeable future as they had been during World
War II. These Cassandras shook their heads dolefully and
made further predictions of a haircurling new depression to
follow the big war.

The big depression didn't happen. Neither did the predicted
moratorium on millionaires.

The comings and goings of millionaires should, it would
seem, be of interest only to themselves and to their well-heeled

brothers. But this is not so. If it had indeed become impossible for new people to join the select ranks of the seven-figured tycoons, then monetary mobility would have left us for good and a worthwhile piece of the American dream would have died.

Happily, more new fortunes have been made in the period that followed World War II than in all of the history of North America previous to that.

This book will tell you how some of those fortunes were made, despite high taxation, despite other obstacles, despite the unrest, social revolution, and industrial and marketing changes that have swept the land.

It will tell how *you* can achieve wealth.

You will learn how great fortunes have been made in common stocks, and how the newest, growingest financial phenomenon, mutual funds, can be made into a road to wealth. It will examine three different ways to ride the real estate road. You will read about the franchising, commodity trading, and merger–acquisition roads. It will tell how those seemingly stodgy things, bonds, can at a right time be made into rapid builders of personal wealth.

An old adage states that money won't buy happiness. This may be true but, as a comedian said, it certainly helps. The wealth to which these nine roads lead will certainly bring satisfaction and a tremendous sense of personal achievement—psychological wealth. In a troubled age, most of us could use a wide measure of that kind of wealth too.

David L. Markstein

Contents

1

Leverage! That's the Trick

I RECALL driving some years ago on a vacation in Florida. We were on a pretty but primitive road that wound beside the Gulf of Mexico where travelers could watch the incoming rollers break on one of Florida's incredibly fine, white sand beaches. Suddenly the car air conditioner went out.

If you are a pampered city type such as I am; the day is a hot July number; the place is a hot Florida beach; and there is no town for six or seven miles in either direction, then the loss of automobile air conditioning looks almost like a tragedy. We pulled to the shoulder of the road to see what could be done.

It was when we set out to find someone more knowledgeable in the next town that a difficulty arose. At the side of the road a big rock blocked the left front wheel. My son tried to move it. No luck. He and I tried together, but it wouldn't budge. Ordinary muscle power was not the answer.

Then a pole was brought. We put one end of the pole under our obstacle, the middle of the pole atop a smaller rock brought up to serve as fulcrum, and the stone that had refused to move when unaided muscle power was applied to it moved very easily with pressure of the pole.

We had employed *leverage*.

Leverage is a means to multiply power and to bring about increased means of accomplishing the same purpose.

Leverage is the key to making a fortune today. It has been the common denominator in just about every fortune-building plan of the last two decades. Our grandfathers believed strongly in the Horatio Alger virtues of hard work, dedication to duty, and avoidance of debt. Hard work is necessary to make anything succeed, and a good sense of duty is an asset to any of us who want to make a career outside the Mafia. (Some say it is even more necessary to success there.) But avoidance of debt? Perhaps this horror of owing money or utilizing others' funds to build fortunes that neither those others nor ourselves could build alone—perhaps that was the reason there were fewer millionaires in our granddads' times than there are today.

Financial leverage is the use of debt to help erect estates that our own sometimes meager moneys could not compile alone.

Leverage has been used in the amassing of almost every fortune in the years since World War II ended.

It is the continuing factor of the Nine Roads to Wealth you will shortly be examining in chapters that follow. Let's look at leverage itself and see if we can grasp something of the nature of the critter, since to try to ride a steed one doesn't know, with whose gaits and good and bad habits one is unfamiliar, can mean a quick trip to disaster—financially and emotionally.

A simple monetary manifestation of leverage is a mortgage. You buy a house. It might cost $30,000. But you don't have $30,000. You do have $3,800, and with this you go to a lender and in effect say: "Give me a loan of $26,200 which I will put up my $30,000 home to secure. I will then pay you back using part of my salary every month during the next twenty years."

Utilizing basic, unsophisticated leverage like this, all of us who have only moderate savings are enabled to swing purchases of homes we could not begin to touch unless we used someone else's money to do it. That someone else is compensated by an interest charge. The borrower pays to rent his capital, just as rent is paid on an apartment in which our hypothetical house buyer might have lived before he decided to join the ranks of the homeowners and begin to enjoy what one wit has termed the privilege of paying for repairs instead of waiting for a landlord to do them.

Consider another kind of leverage. You are certain that a stock called Moon Land Sales is going to boom because it has an option on all livable area of the moon. A big spaceship is just about to blast off with hundreds of colonists eager to buy home sites where things are less crowded and they will not have to fight freeways each evening.

You possess $4,000. Moon Land Sales is listed on the New York Stock Exchange and trading at 40. That means you can buy 100 shares, not counting the commission cost to purchase them. You are so sure that Moon Land is going to be a hotshot high flyer that you would like to swing more shares. But how?

The rock stands before you. It consists of limited ability to participate in a situation you are sure will work out. So you bring up the pole of leverage. In 1969, at the time I write the words you are reading, you could borrow 20 percent of the cost of shares. (The Federal Reserve Board lays down margin requirements which, in the last two decades, have varied from 50 to 100 percent depending upon what the Fed's financial fathers, in their wisdom, consider good for the country at any particular stage of its inflation and deflation cycles.)

Thus by applying a simple kind of margin pole to the rock, you can exert power over 100 shares, not for $4,000, but for $3,200. Or you can use your full $4,000 capital and swing 125 shares on 80 percent margin downpayment. That may not sound like a great deal of leverage, but in a later chapter on stock market leverage we will see ways to exert leverage many times greater than that of a simple margin operation like this. But you will have vastly increased your ability to profit from sales of moon soil to eager colonists should those colonists, as you expect, go all out to establish themselves up on the moon.

Let's suppose you turn out to be correct. The stock of Moon Land Sales shoots up from 40 to 50, to 60, to 80, and at 100 you decide to take your profits and sell. If you had purchased a simple 100 shares, you would be counting some $6,000 of profits in your hot hands and happily announcing to friends that you had made a 150 percent gain atop your original capital. Quite a respectable showing. But if you had swung 125 shares instead of 100, your profit would be $8,500—an extra $2,500 gain—and a whooping percentage leap of 212.5.

That assumes only simple margin leverage of 20 percent. If the Fed happened to allow 30 percent, as it frequently has, the gain would have been correspondingly greater.

Consider another kind of rock.

You own an eating establishment in which you use a special kind of clam juice formula to flavor steaks. The citizens of your town seem to find these superior to steaks cooked in ordinary ways. Your restaurant is crowded. You want to capitalize on it.

"Sorry, George," your accountant says when you talk to him about possibilities of using your capital to open added outlets of George's Clam Juice Steak House. "After taking provision for taxes and keeping aside enough to take care of running expenses we expect will crop up over the next few months, and after seeing to other smaller money needs, you just don't have enough dough to go it big right now. Would you settle for an upstairs addition to the present restaurant?"

You wouldn't. So here is a rock. You need a pole. But what kind? You have talked to the local banker who appears uneager to advance big sums of money for expansion and points out that you lack collateral to protect his depositors whose green stuff you want to borrow. "Why not be a careful fellow," he asks in his friendliest banker style, "and settle for an upstairs addition to your restaurant? We would lend money for that if you give a second mortgage on the building."

That lever obviously isn't strong enough.

But there exists a lever which can do the job. One day after completion of the simple upstairs addition, a customer comes into your office smacking his lips and says something like this:

"I'm Donald Doe from the Doe Worldwide Franchises. You have a good thing going. Have you ever considered the possibilities of franchising it into a national, maybe even an international, organization?"

Out of ensuing conversations with Donald Doe and other members of the Doe organization grows a plan for expanding as quickly as Topsy in the novel or Kentucky Fried Chicken in real life. Soon the franchising lever—which will be examined in detail in a subsequent chapter—has not only removed the rock of monetary inability from the path of expansion, but flipped it clean out of sight.

Leverage is wonderful.

But the day could come when, even after George's Clam Juice Steak Houses dot every landscape and stand on every important corner in nearly every North American town, you might still need money.

"Lookee," you say to the accountant, now grown some years

older, somewhat paunchier, a good deal richer, and considerably sharper in the ways of making other people's money work for his clients. "I have a new process. I want to set up a big computerized operation for everybody in the food business. It will have every client's cost figures, margins, etc., programmed in, and food executives all over the country could have up-to-the-minute operating facts from each one of their outlets at the flick of a terminal button. That isn't something I can franchise. How do I get capital to do it?

"Easy, George," says the CPA. "We'll sell some of the stores that the company instead of its franchisees owns, lease them right back again on long-term arrangements, and I think I can have a couple of million on hand for your fast food computer. Say tomorrow afternoon at four?"

Leasing is another powerful lever which can be applied to flip aside rocks of financial impotence. It can be applied to little rocks as well as big ones and in many other ways than the simple sale-leaseback described above. Leasing's potential to free capital will be discussed in one of the chapters which lies ahead.

Several years pass for you. George's Fast Food Computer is now nearly as big a success as George's Clam Juice Steak House, which can be found in Europe, Japan, and Australia as well as in the North American countries, and which are expanding into parts of Central and South America as "Jorge's Clam Juice Biftek Casas."

You meet the CPA for lunch. He is now known as a financial advisor and limits his conversation to the very rich, a classification which happily has come to include you. "Another problem," you tell him. "The day is coming when I'll want to retire. How can we get some of the money out of the clam juice steak houses and the food service data computer while still exercising control? How can I establish some values for my holdings to benefit my children later on?"

"Let's see," he muses. "We have consulted the leasing lever-age people and the people who make franchising leverage work. How about the going public people?"

Going public is another way of exerting leverage on a finan-cial problem and making others' money work for you. Shortly afterwards you find an underwriting arranged, and presto— your stock, called "George's Consolidated," is soon trading merrily in the over-the-counter market and due to be listed on the American Stock Exchange. While still exercising control, you have received many public dollars for a part of your hold-ings and established a market value for the rest. Now *your* money goes looking for somebody else's small proposition in which it can pry rocks from the paths of success.

We will look in a later chapter at going public as well as other ways of directly financing operations.

We will also look at plays in the stock market; in seemingly staid bonds; in mutual funds; in raw land; in urban improve-ment; in the building, buying, leasing, and selling for profit of apartments and offices; and at commodities; franchising; leas-ing; acquisitions; and mergers.

You can work any of these without leverage. But apply le-verage, and the results might become spectacular instead of merely satisfactory.

It is important, however, to understand leverage before be-ginning to exert it because financial leverage used wrongly has the capability of sending the rock atop your own head instead of removing it from the road, thus worsening instead of im-proving your situation.

Any plan to which leverage is applied must be researched, examined, poked into, and pored over more carefully than in-vestments entered for strict cash. If you read things wrongly, or if a danger should arise that was unforeseen by you—an ex-ample might be discovery that clam juice combined with beef-steak causes warts or makes hair turn blue—then your leverage might make you, instead of the rock, flip into the air and land in a trash heap beside the road you had hoped would lead on to fortune.

Go back a moment to the time when Donald Doe of the Doe Worldwide Franchises organization walked into your office, smiling contentedly after a clam-juice-flavored steak dinner. You and the Doe people agree on terms. You will need something to start the ball rolling, however, and to get it you arrange mortgages on everything around on which lenders will give loans. This might even include a mortgage on your home and loans on your two cars if you are particularly enthusiastic about the potential and happen to be a man ready to plunge everything into a new enterprise.

Joyfully, you watch the franchising operations proceed apace. Advertising, guided by Doe experts, brings in entrepreneurs interested in franchises for their own George's Clam Juice Steak Houses. These are screened with care by Doe's people, brought to your headquarters for training, and construction—financed by *their* money, not yours—begins on eight new Houses in as many cities. The day comes when these open with a mighty fanfare of advertising to proclaim the succulent merits of the clam juice-flavored beefsteak.

Crowds show up.

The next day the crowds are thinner.

At the end of two weeks, the crowds, despite continued advertising, become a trickle.

Your franchisees aren't making money, and so they have no percentage of profits to pay to you.

The bankers, mortgage people, and friendly finance companies send in their notices when your note payments come due.

There isn't enough to pay it all. You had counted on the success of franchised George's Clam Juice Steak Houses. But a liking for clam juice with steaks is purely local. In other sections of the country, people turned up their noses at the unusual taste, said "Yuck!" and advised their friends to stay away from the George's outlets. This the friends did in droves, crowds, mobs, and hordes.

You are broke. Busted. Unable to meet notes out of profits from the still-booming original George's even with its wildly successful upstairs addition. And so into the debt bucket go your real estate, equipment, and perhaps your cars and your home.

No chance for trying out the George's Fast Food Computer idea now. No publicly owned George's Consolidated with a high-flying glamour stock bubbling and trading merrily over-the-counter or on the American Stock Exchange.

Just broke George.

"You should have listened and been content with your up-stairs addition," says the banker consolingly after his loan department people have sold many of your possessions on the courtroom auction block.

Leverage, alas, can wreck as well as build. It behooves you, therefore, to be doubly, triply, maybe quintuply sure of what you are doing before you apply the leverage pole to any financial rock which is blocking your path.

There are other kinds of dangers to leverage. These are none the less real because they are psychological rather than monetary.

If you happen to be a George who worries about things, it might be better for you to use a little pole instead of a big one. Open fewer franchised outlets, and wait for these to succeed before opening more, should you be a man who finds sleep difficult after the days when there have been setbacks. Stock market people have a saying for this kind of psychological danger. "When your stocks make you lose sleep," runs the old Wall Street adage, "sell them down to the sleeping point."

I recall one man who came distractedly into my office. "I'm stuck with all this real estate," he said, listing lot after lot and house after house in a recital which made it plain that he was a very wealthy man indeed, "and now they are going to make money tighter in the country. What shall I do? I owe on every piece of property. It can wreck me. Suppose nobody buys?"

It is a fact that easier money conditions always follow tightening of the financial screw by the Federal Reserve, and if this man did not sell some pieces until tomorrow, he would not go broke today. But these were not the needed words since my client's problems were psychological rather than actual. I suggested immediate sale of some lots before conditions got tighter. He proved happier with fewer holdings and a heftier (if unworking) bank account to ride out the temporary spasm of tight money.

There are rules which, if followed, can save you from both the actual and the psychological dangers that pop up when people employ leverage to whomp up added financial muscle. Hopefully, they should magnify your gains, not your losses.

1. Do Your Homework First   Americans are optimists. That is one of our attractive traits. But optimism can lead you astray if you look only at the good sides of a new venture, and if financial leverage power is applied to that venture—as it should be in all nine of the Roads to Wealth which follow.

"I always ask myself, 'what *if*?' when I consider a new situation in which I might invest," a highly successful Wall Streeter once told me. "What *if* my appraisal of a probable market for the company's products proved wrong by 10 percent? By 20 percent? By 30 percent? How much error would it take to turn a profitable prospect into a dismal sea of red ink?

"Then I ask, 'What are chances of an "if" event happening?' I call this appraising the possibilities as well as the probabilities, and it is startling to see how often what I had considered probabilities aren't probable at all—sometimes they are barely possible—while the adverse possibilities turn out to be probabilities instead."

2. Don't Plunge   I watched a man with the dice in Las Vegas one night. He had only a small stake to start. He doubled that, then let the pile ride on every bet. For a few times he won, and his profits began to look tremendous. Then the dice went against him and he was broke.

There is a lesson in this.

The lesson is that in business or in gambling, it does not pay to bet everything every time. Plungers look good when they succeed. However, since a plunger can't be wrong even one time, and since few of us are infallible or so lucky that we can expect things to go our own way every time out, then the plunger is bankrupt the first time the dice, or the business cycle, go against him. Leverage can make this kind of instant failure awesomely final.

It generally pays to hold something back. Then if you are proved wrong, you have a stake left with which to try the Road to Wealth again.

If you prove successful, such kicker capital can serve as extra muscle to be applied to the pole *after* the pole has begun to move the obstacle away. After the first try has proved successful, you'll have more money to buy more leverage to follow up early success.

3. *Plan in Advance How You Will Cut Losses* Truly successful travelers on the nine Roads to Wealth which will be detailed in coming chapters are those with enough humility to know that there is always a chance of being wrong, and that new, impossible-to-foresee conditions may have made the original calculations incorrect. In these cases, it pays to cut losses, save what is left after the initial setback, and get out.

Before entering on any project detailed here, decide in advance just where you will cry "Halt!"; how you will get out; and where along the road you will turn back for a fresh beginning.

4. *Caveat Is a Latin Word—It Means Beware!* You should beware of one trap that leverage holds—the trap of becoming overenthusiastic so that you commit money which should be held back for family security. Before you embark on one of the nine leveraged ways to wealth you should have adequate insurance, your home equity should not be endangered, and your savings account should be reasonably hefty so that if an emergency arose you would be able to take care of it.

TO RECAP:

1. Leverage is the multiplying of force. It can multiply muscle power, weight energy—or money. Most big fortunes in the post–World War II years have been made with the help of leverage.

2. In its simplest form, leverage calls for using others' funds to supplement your own, so that if a project is successful the effect will be multiplied by profits made on borrowed money or money released from other uses.

3. But leverage can work both ways. It can add to losses if an investment or a business idea goes wrong. Wise travelers on the Roads to Wealth therefore look carefully up and down, and they examine the vehicles they intend to ride before they set out, lest leverage's force be employed against them instead of working in their favor.

4. Leverage is the common denominator of all of the Roads to Wealth described in this book. It can be found in the forms of margin, franchise financing, leasing, mortgaging, and all kinds and manners of employing money belonging to others for your profit—and theirs.

2

Multiply the Gains from Winning Stocks

IF YOU WERE to glance down from the visitors' gallery at the confused floor of the New York Stock Exchange, you would see scores of men bustling about a place that looks like an airplane hangar in which posts have been placed at intervals. Yet the NYSE is the financial capital of the world. It is the place where, probably, more new fortunes are made every year and old fortunes lost, than in any other spot on earth.

Its liquidity allows you to enter a situation in the morning and sell out of it in the afternoon should you change your mind over the before-lunch martinis. Nor is it necessary to look beyond this place if you desire strong leverage, for here so many kinds of leverage can be exerted that a push on the pole can put out 50 percent, 100 percent, sometimes 200 percent to 500 percent of your actual financial weight.

There is also the nearby American Stock Exchange where a great deal of the rapid action happens. And there is a still faster market, unorganized but efficient, in which over-the-counter dealers handle volatile, leveraged securities and in which a number of the springiest, strongest leverage poles are to be found.

Let's take a moment to define stocks, bonds, convertibles, warrants, and Puts and Calls. Common stocks (also sometimes called "capital stocks" or referred to in generic terms as "equities") are shares of ownership in a corporation.

While a stockholder is one of the owners of a corporation, a bondholder is one of its creditors. A bond is an enormously complicated kind of I O U. Some bonds are known as "mortgage bonds." These have for security the property of the corporation which, in the event of default, bondholders are supposed to be able to sell on the auction block to get their money back. In practice this seldom happens. Other bonds are "revenue bonds." Certain kinds of revenue are dedicated to servicing the bonds by providing for interest and building of a fund to eventually pay them off when they come due. A third breed of bonds is called "debentures." These are unsecured.

Preferred stock is a hybrid kind of security. Holders of preferred must be paid a set dividend before anything can be paid on the common. But preferred stockholders come after the bondholders in getting a share in any breakup of a company. A few preferred issues "participate" by being paid the same dividends as common in addition to their set yield.

Warrants are options to buy stock at a set price. Most warrants expire eventually but a few are perpetual.

Another kind of option is the Put or Call. You pay money to buy a Put which allows you to tender stock at a set price to the seller of the Put. Calls are the opposite of Puts; they allow you to call for, or buy, stock at a predetermined price. Put and Call options always have close-in expiration dates and are not issued by a corporation as are securities above, but by another investor who works through a Put and Call dealer.

Those, then, are the instruments around which aggressive investors attempt to lever their way to wealth. Bonds will be examined in a chapter that follows. All of the others, however, become good plays or bad plays because of the merit of a common stock. Therefore, let's look at what makes a common stock inviting to buy.

Investors traditionally have one of three reasons for buying securities. The first is to preserve their dollars. We will rule that one out since our object is to build wealth, not to conserve wealth which already exists. A second objective is to secure high income. The building of a big estate comes only slowly to a fellow who patiently plows back his 4 percent, 5 percent or 6 percent dividends, so we will discard that motive, too, from consideration.

The third objective is to make capital itself grow, with only secondary attention to whether it produces a current yield and how big or little that yield might be.

That is the way we will look at stocks. Have they the potential to grow? Soon? To what degree?

Three kinds of stocks can produce rapid capital growth. First is the "growth stock," a loose term which Wall Streeters misuse as often as they use it correctly and which we will attempt to define down to sharp terms to help you choose really growing situations around which to employ leverage methods.

All kinds of criteria have been devised for separating true growth stocks from the stocks whose growth is only seeming. One is a formula—it looks complicated but can be worked in minutes—that I call the Growth Performance Yardstick. Here it is:

$$SG \times EG \times DG \times PG + IG + OPC - PER \times S \times FP = \text{Performance Rating}$$

SG—sales growth: This indicates how the overall sales of a company have grown in ten years.

EG—earnings growth per share: Represents the per share earnings growth of the company in question during the same ten-year period.

DG—dividend growth: Indicates the growth in dividends paid to shareholders during the ten-year period.

PG—price growth: This is measured from the high of ten years ago to the high of the current year.

IG—industry growth: On the average, the stock of a company in a growing industry stands a better chance of appreciation. Of course an aggressive company may grow in any industry. A numerical factor of one to four is assigned here.

OPC—outperforming competition: The ability to outperform competition, as indicated by past history and probable future experience, is rated from one to four.

PER—price-earnings ratio: When price is too high in ratio to earnings, a price weakness may develop. So this is subtracted from the formula.

S—stability: Ratings from one to four are assigned, based upon constantly updated judgment.

FP—future prospects: A rating from one to four is assigned on the basis of likely future growth and prosperity.

There is no one "right" answer to this equation. In Wall Street as in so much of life, things are comparative. However, when you apply the Growth Performance Yardstick to two or more stocks it will quickly show which is cheapest on an earnings basis and in which of the stocks all factors combine to give a probably best choice.

Let's do some sample arithmetic: We will look at National Can Corp., a staid but steady doyen of the growth stock clan, and National Steel Corp., a most meritorious company but one which is seldom described by the adjective "growth."

In ten years through the end of 1968, sales growth of National Can was 2.6 times the starting figure. Earnings growth was even better; the per share profits popped up 10.4 times the figure of ten years earlier. Dividend growth almost kept pace at 6.7 times. Price growth was 6.3. Performing the necessary multiplication gives a figure of 1,139.67.

The price-earnings ratio ran 15 at the price when this computation was made. Subtracting that gave 1,124.67, which was first multiplied by the arbitrary stability rating of 3 based upon National Can's record and the steadiness of its industry, and then by the future prospects rating of 3 which was also assigned arbitrarily. The result was a growth performance rating of 10,119.

National Steel's sales grew 2.1 times, but its earnings growth was not as spectacular as that of National Can. It ran 1.93 times the starting figure of ten years earlier. The dividend growth was 1.66 and price growth 1.3 times. Multiplying these by each other gave a number of 8.8. The price earnings ratio, alas, was 9.2 at the time, and so the necessary subtraction of 9.2 from 8.8 resulted in a negative number. A minus times anything is still a minus; therefore despite an arbitrarily assigned stability rating of 2.0 and a future prospects rating of 1.5, National Steel's growth performance rating was minus.

Professional investment people call the second kind of potentially profitable stock a "turnaround situation." A turnaround happens when a new factor is added to an old, stale profits mix. Such a stock frequently has explosive potential for rapid growth. The turnaround situation's new factor might be a changed economic atmosphere in which its product is in sudden demand. It might be a management team coming in to replace old, stodgy leaders of the corporation. It might be a bent in a new direction which promises better results than the older ways of doing things. Frequently, turnaround situations come about because of better ways of producing or selling the same goods. Turnarounds can be enormously profitable. But they have led some investors down the garden path to nowhere instead of onto the Road to

Wealth because change—any change—became heralded as a turn for the better when in some cases it meant only continued profits stagnation despite new factors.

In early 1968 some observant investors noted that a turnaround had taken place in an American Stock Exchange company called Interstate United where new management with fresh ideas was making profits zoom like a rocket. Suddenly, earnings jumped from a deficit of $1.54 to a black ink profit the next year of 22 cents. The following year profits were 52 cents per share, and they moved down to 47 cents, then to 98 cents. By 1968, the turnaround process had been several years in progress. Yet the stock, purchasable at 12 in early January, was selling at a lofty 38 by the end of the year.

Similarly, earnings per share of Monroe Auto Equipment flopped and floundered for several years until 1966, when the figure jumped suddenly from 92 cents to $1.70. Skeptical analysts and investors did nothing until, in 1967, the earnings jumped again to $2.71. By the end of 1967, the turnaround had been well established. Despite the fact that this seemed late in the game, commitments made in the stock then at 29 looked very good by spring, 1969, when, even though there had been a decline in the overall market, Monroe stock was above 70 (before a 2-for-1 split).

Such results can be had in correctly diagnosed turnarounds.

Turnaround situations are to be found during all years. One successful searcher after turnarounds explained his method to me:

> I watch every new factor that comes into a company picture —new management, new products, new conditions. But I don't act until the new factor has already proved itself by producing better results. The buying conditions are generally still good even then, for unbelief generated by the company's old performance leads most people watching the stock to shrug off the gain as a temporary thing. By the time I am ready, such unbelief usually still exists. It is when unbelief yields to enthusiasm that a stock rise—the thing for which I have bought—usually occurs.

Another profitable stock is the special situation. There a factor exists which can push up price regardless of general market trend. Frequently, special situations are uncovered when an investor spots a something which the market as a whole has not yet noticed. An example was the existence of hungry merger appetites of some conglomerates which, in 1968, were beginning to feed upon paper companies because of the low multiples of these companies and the capacity for new growth in paper demand.

One of the real experts on the special situation is Arnold M. Ganz, vice-president of Delaware Management Co. which manages the Delaware Mutual Fund. In an article in *Investment Sales Monthly* of September, 1966, Mr. Ganz explained the technique:

> What is a special situation? *A special situation is an investment likely to have minimum calculable downside price risk and factors not generally recognized by investors, and is likely to result in capital appreciation. It is the minimum downside risk and lack of investor recognition that makes the situation a special one—not the fact that it is someone's favorite stock.*
>
> Minimum calculable downside risk is sometimes created by yield, in the form of dividends or interest. Yield, to support the market price, must be analyzed carefully to assure the investors that the current dividend or interest payments are safe. . . . Asset protection provides another downside stop. Either the market price of the security is low in relation to its book value, or it sells at a substantial discount from its net working capital, or assets on the balance sheet are understated. The special situations analyst must assure himself that the book value on the balance sheet is real, valuable, and likely to be used to better advantage by management in the future. An additional downside stop exists in non-recognized securities. A company may go unnoticed because of a lack of publicity or sponsorship. Its stock price may be substantially lower than others of its kind due to a lack of investor recognition, and this can provide a significant downside stop.
>
> A favorite class of special situations encompasses those issues having great statistical attraction and, in addition, a substantial plus factor which could potentially produce a sizeable capital

gain. General Tire & Rubber is a classic example. The year was 1958; the price was $27; the price-earnings ratio was very low. Careful analysis indicated the market price was cheap relative to other securities in the same basic industry. In addition, General Tire controlled Aerojet, then a fledgling, but burgeoning, rocket company. The investor, by buying General Tire, received Aerojet "for free."

Say that tomorrow morning your favorite market letter writer comes up with a pip of a special situation, or perhaps your broker calls to say, "Hey, George! I have just the thing for you"—and then proceeds to outline a doozy of a growth stock situation, still reasonably priced.

What do you do? Buy the stock?

Not if you are a leverage-minded investor who wants to make each of his limited dollars do the work of two or three additional bucks so that leverage can magnify a reasonable profit into a real whopper of a gain.

Let's watch as George, our leverage hound, searches for a pole to swing extra dollar power in an investment he feels sure will go to the moon.

"Okay, Harry," he says to the broker. "I'm sold on the story. Now tell me about the capitalization. Any warrants outstanding?"

Since this is a young swinger of a corporation it has, in common with so many other young swingers today, an issue of warrants which can be used to buy stock at 20. The stock is now 19. The warrants sell for 3. As George's broker explains the figures, this would indicate that he has to pay a premium of $4 to buy the warrant instead of the stock.

Buy the stock?

Or buy the warrant?

George orders 100 shares of stock plus 500 warrants.

In a leverage play like this homework must be carefully done in advance and checked minutely by the investor before he buys. If the stock does not appreciate as expected, there will be a loss on the stock purchase plus a correspondingly greater percentage loss of money put into the warrants. George knows this and has done his advance work with care.

The stock performs as expected.

Earnings shoot up from last year's $1.50 per share. In the first quarter of the fiscal year, the company earns 53 cents versus 30 cents last year. Analysts perk up and take notice. The stock begins to ascend. When the second quarter's report shows earnings equal to the previous year's in only half the elapsed time, the stock does indeed reach for the moon, jumping from 20 to 25, to 30, 35, 38, and by the time George has held it six months and a day (the time necessary under income tax regulations to make any gain long term rather than ordinary income) the stock is selling at 43. Still at a premium of 4, the warrants now sell at 27.

George gives the order to sell his 100 shares plus 400 of his 500 warrants. "I'll just hang on to the last 100 warrants as a kicker," he tells the broker. "What can I lose? This is all gravy now."

George's investment was $3,400 (plus commissions which are omitted here for the sake of easy calculation, but which might have been balanced off by George's receipt of two dividend checks). Counting up the dollars received from sale of 400 warrants at 27 and 100 shares of stock at 43, George found he had a total of $15,100. "And I still have 100 warrants going for me, at zero cost," he boasted to a friend. "If the stock shoots up still more I won't be altogether out of things; my warrants ought to add up to a further profit."

On the stock George made a $2,400 profit from a $1,900 investment, a neat 127 percent gain. On his warrants—the swinging, leveraged part of the play—he made (not giving any value to the 100 warrants still riding) $9,300 on a $1,500 investment. "That's 625 percent," he reported to his somewhat awed friend. "Leverage play is certainly the way to make it!"

Not all stocks have warrants on which a money-multiplying

play like this can be based. But Put and Call options are available on nearly any listed stock.

If there were no warrants, George's conversation with his broker might have gone like this:

"Okay, wire New York. I want to know how much a Call of six months ten days will cost." Six-month ten-day periods are commonly used in option trading, and back might come the quote: "Stock at 19. Calls available six months ten days for $250 per 100 shares."

If in such a case George were to make the same kind of play he made in warrants, but utilizing Calls instead, and if the price action had proceeded as outlined earlier, his profit picture might have looked something like this:

Cost to acquire 100 shares outright at 19	$ 1,900
Cost to acquire 5 100-share Calls at 250	1,250
Total cost	$ 3,150
Proceeds from 100 shares sold at 43	$ 4,300
Proceeds, purchase of 500 shares via Call at 19, and sale of these shares at 43	20,250
Total proceeds	$24,550

Although this profit looks and is whoppingly large, it is well to note a few differences between leverage trading via warrants and leveraged investment using Calls. Greater capital is required for Put and Call trading. In the case of the warrants, George's cost was confined to the price of the warrant itself, and when he sold it was not necessary for him to "exercise" the warrant by purchasing stock. He sold the warrant itself.

Although markets sometimes exist for selling a Call, these are neither very liquid nor present all of the time. The usual procedure is to do what George was compelled to do: use the Call to purchase stock at the option price of 19, then sell the newly bought stock at the market price of 43. This requires greater capital and hence reduced the percentage of profit made on the transaction. The Put and Call pole is not as long as the warrant pole and exerts less monetary magnification.

Moreover, the loss using Calls could have been the total amount employed should George's judgment have been incorrect with the stock declining. A warrant always continues to have some value. But on the day it expires a Call is as dead as the dinosaur. If the stock stays at its same level, loss on a Call is total. On the other hand, the loss could not at any time have been greater than the $1,250 which George paid to buy the options.

Put and Call options are bought through any regular New York Stock Exchange member firm and can be obtained from other dealers.

George's procedure with Calls was to buy them. Other people increase the leverage from stocks by "writing" (or selling) options.

Assume that George had bought 100 shares and was able to play the warrant game outlined in the first instance. Now the stock is 43. George sells his warrants but retains the stock. He then approaches his broker.

"We've made a pretty profit on the warrants and I still have the stock. I have such a handsome profit on the whole deal that we might say the stock costs nothing as things stand. Of course the tax collectors won't look at it that way, but for my own purposes it is true. Now let's wring some more money out of the situation. Arrange for me to write a Call on it."

Working through a Put and Call dealer, George's broker puts together a deal whereby George stands willing to sell 100 shares of Groovy Growth at the existing 43 to any investor who holds the Call. For this he might receive about $400 after the broker and option dealer have extracted their commissions.

Groovy Growth goes down. So the option remains unexercised (SEC figures showed that in a recent year a majority of such options did expire just this way). Now George has lost some of his gain in the stock itself but is ahead by what he received for writing the Call. Moreover, he still possesses the stock.

Suppose that instead of declining, Groovy Growth ascends to 53. George is called for the stock and duly delivers. "See," he says to broker Harry as he hands over the endorsed certificate, "if I had sold the stock at 43, I would have received $400 less."

(Sometimes speculators in George's shoes retain a *warrant* for 100 shares to be exercised if called upon to deliver stock. George, a conservative swinger, chose to hold the stock itself. Perhaps he admired the light blue ink in which its corners were printed.)

With warrant usage to multiply leverage, George might have increased his money magnification still more by using the allowable margin on both stock and warrants and with the Put and Call play might have employed margin on purchase of the stock itself.

"Margin" is expressed in percentages. These vary. They have been as low as 50 percent during the post–World War II years. If you were told you could buy Groovy Growth at 20 percent margin, that would mean you had to put up 80 cents for every dollar's value of stocks you bought. Employing margin on Groovy Growth—both on warrants and stock—could have increased George's profit thus:

■ $1,900 capital employed to buy 100 shares outright would have bought 125 shares on 80 percent prevailing margin. On this he would have received $5,375 when the stock was sold, instead of $4,300. His profit on the stock itself, exclusive of warrants which we will look at separately, would have been $3,475 or 183 percent atop his original capital employed for stock.

■ Instead of buying 500 warrants at 3, the same $1,500 capital for warrant purchasing could swing 625 warrants. Retaining 100 of these as in the original example, George would sell 525 warrants at 27 to receive $14,175.

■ Investing the same $3,400 total amount in stock and warrants would have enabled George, now using margin to additionally leverage the leverage he already had from warrants, to count up $19,550 total receipts. "This," he told his friend Ronald over the third scotch and water that evening in a neighborhood tavern and pizza palace, "is $4,450 extra profit. People ask what you can do with such meager margin opportunities as the Fed offers today. I added an extra 130 percent gain by using the margin to put a kicker onto a situation already leveraged."

Margin requirements add interest to a form of security known as "convertibles." Some "converts" are bonds. These are generally debentures. Others are preferred stocks. In each case, there is a price at which the conversion can be made. Say that your convert is a $1,000 debenture bond. Say that it can be changed into common stock at 24½ face value. This was the case with debentures of a Southwestern natural resource company which came out early in spring, 1969, and were eagerly gobbled up by investors interested in both the high yield and growth prospects.

In this case, for each $1,000 bond you could buy 40 shares of stock and have $20 cash left as change. Bonds sell at commissions much lower than the percentages assessed on stock purchases. You would pay nothing to convert into common should you decide to do so. Therefore you would save considerable commission.

The bond is convertible at 24½. The stock is trading at the moment at 22½. "Why would you want to buy the debenture?" a skeptical friend asked George. "Seems to me it would be cheaper to buy the common at two bucks under conversion price."

"True," says George. "But consider some arithmetic. The common stock pays 40 cents a year right now. That is a meager 1¾ percent return. The convertible debenture at par pays 5¾. The difference is 4 percent added income. I might buy 45 shares of common, each paying me 40 cents, and I would have an income of $18 per year. But if I bought the bond I would receive $57.50 return on every thousand dollar bill laid out. For that, I can wait out the two points since I am convinced the stock will go up. If it does, the debenture has to rise in proportion to the stock once the conversion price has been passed. In practice, the debenture is likely to begin rising before the parity comes, staying at a premium. And that is not all.

"I have a lot more downside protection in the convertible. Suppose the stock of the company were to go down. The debenture has a price at which it is likely to sell on the basis of yield, since some people will buy it just for that purpose without regard to growth potential of the convertible feature. So I have downside protection I would not have in the stock."

But the real advantage, as George knew, was spelled l-e-v-e-r-a-g-e.

While Federal Reserve margin requirements of early 1969 spelled out 80 percent downpayment requirement on credit purchases of common stocks, the same Fed allowed 60 percent margin for convertible bonds.

Assume that George buys 100 shares at 22½. His judgment proves to be correct. Before a year is out the stock has risen ten points. George's profit: $1,000.

But being leverage-minded, George, instead of buying 100 shares outright, purchases 125 on margin for about the same amount of capital. His profit then becomes $1,250.

Margin used alone in this fashion is not a very large pole. It can only send the smaller rocks springing out of George's path. Casting about for a bigger, springier pole George looks to the 5¾ percent converts.

"Aha!" he says to broker Harry. "Let's buy those. My capital ought to swing about 3¾ bonds. I'll put up an extra hundred and a half and buy a round four of the convertible debentures." (Most bonds, although quoted in hundreds, are issued in $1,000 denominations.)

Probabilities are that if the stock rises ten points the bond will keep edging a little in advance of the stock, maintaining its premium and adding on the same percentage of gain so that ten points profit on the stock would mean about the same profit on the bond.

Tack on 45 percent profit, and the bonds would be selling at $1,450 each. The profit in this case would be $1,800 rather than the $1,250 possible on a margin purchase of the common stock or $1,000 achievable on a straight out-and-out purchase of common with no leverage at all.

Has George by this time exhausted all of the kinds of leverage possible in stocks and things convertible into common stock? He has tried warrants, Puts and Calls, convertible bonds, preferred stocks, and the use of margin to add an additional mite of height to the leverage pole.

There remains the search for companies with *internal* leverage, to which the outside forms of leverage which George has already discovered can be added to achieve what in some cases become awesome money multiplication.

The classic kind of internal leverage is found in a company where (1) a turnaround toward higher profits is expected; (2) there is a high break-even point beyond which profits might bound rapidly upward; or (3) there exists a heavy senior capitalization ahead of the common and until the turnaround, this has eaten up existing corporate profits.

Say that George finds a shoe company which new management has taken over. If his information is correct, this management will produce a genuine turnaround in profits. By the time George considers the stock, the management has already shown evidence of being able to do this, and George decides the company is worth an investment.

High costs, however, continue to plague the company. Some of the machinery is old. Time and additional capital are required to replace it. But once the high break-even point has been passed, nothing stands between the profit figures and the sky but a little atmosphere. There now appears evidence that management has generated enough new sales volume to pierce the overhanging cost barrier. Beyond that barrier, earnings could double this year, triple the next.

It thus takes only a small added sales push to bring about skyrocketing earnings gains. The leverage on *earnings* is very great. Since rising earnings of the sort George expects can result in even more rapidly rising stock prices, George decides that here is a company with true internal leverage.

"But wait a minute before you put everything into this stock," said an advisor. "I've read about another company with the same kind of big internal leverage. Maybe you would like to split your capital between the two."

The second company is also a turnaround situation. Instead of being burdened with heavy and high factory costs, this company has as its legacy from a not very brilliant past management a capital structure with two issues of preferred and some mortgage bonds which must be serviced before money is available to the use of the common stock.

In this second situation lay the same type of leverage as possessed by the shoe manufacturer. Once sales were pushed beyond the point at which profits were needed to pay interest and sinking fund requirements on the mortgage bonds, and had risen past the preferred dividend needs, then earnings per share of common stock might skyrocket.

"Hey, Harry," said George after a study of the numbers. "This one is even better. One of its preferred stock issues is a convert—we can use that, together with margin, to leverage more action out of the same investment."

A last and frequently overlooked kind of leverage is exercised by the price-earnings ratio of a stock. In trying to follow Baron Nathan Rothschild's classic advice on how to get rich in stocks ("Buy low, sell high," he recommended) investors and financial folk run into the problem of determining what is low and what is high. Thus Wall Street has invented the price-earnings ratio. Probably you are familiar with it. If not, here is a brief explanation of how it works:

Say the price of Groovy Growth is 54. The company earned $2.70 per share in the last twelve months. Divide $2.70 into $54.00 and you get 20. That is the price-earnings ratio.

No one knows for certain what is a high ratio and what is a low one. Long ago it was considered smart to buy a stock at a PER of ten or less and pretty dumb to pay a higher multiple for it. The world was simpler in many ways in those easier years. Today, Wall Streeters are aware that a company with fast growth of earnings deserves a higher ratio than plodding old Amalgamated Buggy Whip whose earnings haven't varied 10 cents since McKinley was President.

As a general rule you can say that a company whose earnings are growing is on the cheap side if it sells at a PER of ten or below. If earnings are increasing at any worthwhile clip, PERs of twelve, fifteen, or sixteen remain low. Over twenty you begin to get on the rich side.

George can use the PER as a leverage pole if he spots a situation which, in his opinion, is on the bargain shelf. Real growth and turnaround situations eventually become recognized as such. Then the multiple of earnings tends to get higher. So that if George were to buy Groovy Growth at a multiple of twelve, and then the stock's potential came to the attention of investors at large, George could gain in two ways. Assume earnings of $2.70 are growing at an annual average clip of 15 percent. With the stock at 30, George would be able to watch a 15 percent appreciation in the next year if the multiple stood still. But multiples seldom stand still under such circumstances; it might go to eighteen. Then on earnings of $3.10 ($2.70 plus 15 percent growth) and a price-earnings ratio of eighteen, the stock would sell at 55¾.

TO RECAP:

1. Stock markets where bits and pieces of corporate owner-ship are traded afford you not only maximum liquidity, itself a most important thing, but extremely high leverage so that relatively small sums are able to swing large blocks of stock and produce higher profits when things work as expected.

2. When a company has warrants outstanding, a bigger speculative play can usually (but not always) be made in the warrant. Being lower in cost, but having to go up dollar for dollar with the common, warrants afford extra action for every dollar.

3. Put and Call options can be bought to control a block of a stock at a set price for a predetermined length of time. However, Puts and Calls can expire without ever producing a profit and all of the money invested in them can be lost. Many investors prefer to "write," or sell, Put and Call options.

4. Convertible preferred stocks or debentures allow more leverage because margin requirements are lower on converts than on the underlying common into which they can be changed at owners' options.

5. Companies in which leverage profit plays are usually attempted generally fall into the growth stock, turnaround, or special situation classifications. In each of these, higher prices are expected to come about because of increasing per share earnings.

6. Often, companies have a built-in leverage on earnings. This is particularly true of turnarounds and might be due to the high service costs of a top-heavy senior capitalization of bonds and preferreds ahead of the common or to break-even levels beyond which a small sales push can produce a very large increase in earnings.

7. Leverage is added to a price increase when a growing

stock can be obtained at a low price-earnings ratio. If earnings increase, an added price increase could come about if investors bid for the stock with such vigor as to increase its price-earnings multiple.

8. Margin leverage atop all of these other kinds can add an extra 25 to 66 percent money multiplication.

3

The Bond Bit

Do you believe that bonds are investments fit only for widows, orphans, and that faceless but legally important fellow, the "prudent man"?

Do you think that even high yields accruing under today's conditions make bonds suspect because of inflationary effects, and therefore the investment merits of corporate, municipal, and federal I O U's are miniscule?

Do you believe, as some say, that bonds represent only guaranteed confiscation, if not of the number of dollars involved, at least of their eventual purchasing power?

Do you believe that bond investing is the ploy of yesterday's businessman clad in a high collar and frock coat, but that today's swinger has to have redder meat in the form of stocks, converts, options, and even that far-out gambit of the institutional investor, letter stocks?

There is enough truth in each of these statements to make bonds seem staid, fat, dumpy, sexless, and altogether uninteresting.

But look at bonds instead from a short-swing point of view. Remember that even fat, short, dumpy, sexless, uninteresting women can appear attractive if viewed in just the right light. In that right (and rare) time of the economic day when the light is right, bonds can be as sexy as a bikini-wearing lass with a luscious figure. Then add the glasses of *leverage* to see bonds through and you have, on rare but right occasions, some of the quickest ways to make a little money run into a lot that you will ever find.

Changing the metaphor, if you use the right leverage pole at the correct moment then you can clear—through bonds—a wide and inviting avenue to wealth.

That is what this chapter is all about.

Let's look first at the anatomy of bonds, for there are a great many varieties. In the preceding chapter, we saw the leverage possibilities in employing convertible bonds in place of the common stock into which they can be changed at the owner's will. Convertibles in that kind of speculation were used as a disguised common stock because of higher loan leverage possible when they are bought on margin—also for the higher income they often produce when compared with the stock for which they are a substitute.

The play in this chapter is not in bonds as substitutes for anything, but in the real, solid merits (at certain times) of using that leverage pole to push on the bond market rather than the stock market.

Bonds include:

Treasury bonds. These take in all kinds of government obligations but not, for our purposes as travelers on the leveraged Road to Wealth, savings bonds which are nontransferable. We need the kind of bonds ("marketables") which are bought and sold in an active market that we hope will from time to time swing down to give us the opportunity for getting aboard, then swing up to carry our capital to more profitable levels.

Extremely short-term federal debt instruments are call "bills." These range from three months up to one year. Each Monday, bills are auctioned, and the price at which they go sets the interest rate. Since they lack capital gains attraction, bills are useful mainly as a depository for funds you are holding idle for a short time.

It is the marketable notes and bonds which interest gains-minded investors. Often overlooked in this bond market segment are the "semi-governments" such as Federal Land Bank bonds, Federal National Mortgage Association ("Fannie Mae"), and other securities in the half-land of public sector corporations. These generally carry interest rates higher than regular treasuries. Often their maturities are very short. It is occasionally possible to find at times of extremely tight money such bargains as the Federal Land Bank $4\frac{1}{8}$'s of $\frac{2}{73}$ available in summer, 1969, at 83.8. Translated from Wall Streetese, this meant that a bond of the Federal Land Bank, bearing an interest rate (calculated at par) of $4\frac{1}{8}$ percent and due to be paid off in February, 1973, could be bought at 83.8.

Bonds are generally issued in $1,000 denominations but quoted as if 100 and not 1,000 were par. So this bond, to be redeemed in about three and one-half years in the future at $1,000, was selling for $838. The possible gain was not huge. But when leverage possibilities are considered, plus the fact that the redemption at full par value of $1,000 was about as sure as anything in an unsure world, the bond offered sound speculative possibilities.

Municipal bonds are issued by governing bodies at lower echelons than those in Washington. Municipals include bonds of states, counties, bridge authorities, toll road authorities, and the like as well as those of cities and towns. The income is free of federal income taxation. Often it is also tax-free to investors who live in the state which issued them.

Like treasuries, municipals sink sometimes to unreasonably low levels. When they do, and when an investor additionally has cause to believe the sinking is over and the rise from the slough about to begin, then these present a wonderful leveraged road to a land of better living.

There is a special group of tax-exempt bonds for our purpose less useful than the regular municipals. These are tax-free notes. They are much like treasury bills and, like bills, have attraction chiefly as a haven for funds that you expect to bring back into the speculative battle at no long time hence. A hybrid municipal is the industrial revenue bond. These were issued by communities to finance a plant to be used by an industry attracted to the town, the payoff at maturity guaranteed by the corporation using the plant. Such big names as Fruehauf, Georgia-Pacific, Firestone Tire and Rubber, and U.S. Steel guarantee industrial revenue bonds. The Treasury regards tax exemption of these as a loophole, and in 1968 Congress passed an act limiting the exemption to issues of less than $1 million. However, many issues that came out earlier still trade merrily and attract investors.

Corporates are issued as well as paid off by companies. Some of them are as big and prestigious as U.S. Steel; some operate backyard widget factories.

Prices of bonds vary by the quality of companies issuing them and by the credit ratings of cities and states. Nearly all bond investors accept the ratings given by statistical services although these have no set formulas for bond valuation. Usually, a committee takes into account the size and credit standing of the issuer, the ratio of interest charges to earnings, current assets, current liabilities, etc. Valuing bonds is a subjective process.

Yet ratings given by the two major services, Standard and Poor's and Moody's, will determine into which stratum of bond prices a new issue will fall. Thereafter, the bond is likely to go up or down with others of its grouping. When speculating as to where a depressed bond might go it is well to examine where bonds of similar ratings have sold under the type of money conditions you expect to come about in the close future.

Most investors shy away from even the best-rated bonds as fearfully as they do from the new debenture of Joe's Widget Works which operates out of Joe's attic and carries a credit rating of ZZZ. Of all investors, bond buyers have fared worst over the long years since World War II ended, if long-term results are considered.

But your problem is not twenty-year results. It is to construct a Road to Wealth no more than a year or so in length and preferably a good deal shorter than that.

From the short-term point of view, bond investing has on occasion been a remarkably fine way to get rich.

■ During a recent calendar year American and Foreign Power 5's of 2030 had a high of 73 and a low of 63. The difference was 16 percent profit for an investor who bought low and sold high. If George had borrowed 80 percent on these bonds from his friendly banker, he might have put up $1,260.99 to buy ten. On these he would have realized $1,000 profit if he sold at the top—a neat gain of 70 percent in relatively fast order.

■ From 61 to 69 moved the 2⅞'s of 1987 American Telephone and Telegraph, a top-rated debt instrument whose high rating did not prevent a 13.2 percent fluctuation during twelve recent months.

By leveraging a situation like that, George might have bought ten bonds at 61, using $1,220 and borrowing the remainder from his bank. When the bond moved to 69, George would have realized $800 in profits, a 65.5 percent capital increase.

■ Going down slightly in the bond quality scale, George might have bought the 5's of 1988 of Gordon Jewelry at a low of 105. These moved during the year between that figure and 142. The difference was 36 points or 34.4 percent. This offered even better possibilities with leverage. Buying ten of the Gordon Jewelry bonds at their low, using $2,110 capital of his own and a bank loan of $8,390, George could have counted $3,650 as profit on his $2,110 investment when he closed out the position.

"That's 173 percent gain," he pointed out to an awed Ronald as he paid the tavern tab. "Not many swinging situations can beat bonds if you can manage to catch them right."

■ Lest it appear that bond gains in the instances cited above were hand-picked, the Dow-Jones 40-Bond Average, representing a wide spectrum of bond grades and maturities, would have provided interesting profits if George had been able to buy that average. One recent year saw the D-J Bonds with a high of 85.56 and a low of 74.62. The variation was 10.9 points or 14.7 percent. Add leverage to that, at the generally available amount of 80 percent, and if George had bought the bond average, he would have put up $1,492.40 to buy ten units. On this his profit would have come to $1,094. A 73 percent profit is not to be regarded with scorn.

Once, if an investor were at all skillful at prognosticating stock prices, he had it made for figuring the bond market. Bonds always went in the opposite direction from stocks. If stocks were going down, then bonds were going up. When stocks were on the up trend, then woe to the bond market. A man could always have something working on the upside for him in those simpler days. Now, alas, things are not so simple.

For in the decade of the sixties, inflation caught up with both the bond and stock markets on more than one occasion. Figures show that the pace of inflation accelerated considerably during this decade. The average increase in money supply during the time since the flames of World War II died out was 2.5 percent according to the statistics of the money-smart Federal Reserve Bank of St. Louis. This rate proved sustainable with America's growth in productivity.

But during 1968, when the pace of inflation reached a white heat, money supply grew at around a 6 percent rate. This was not a rate which could be shrugged off.

Two years earlier, the Fed has seen the pace heating up. It tightened its monetary screws. The result was the famous money crunch of 1966. The crunch sent stock market prices spinning downward. 1966 was the second-worst postwar bear market. Bonds, instead of going up, also tumbled because the money tightness which made stockholders fear for corporate prices directly affected bond yields at the same time. Since the Fed was not easing money when the market was down, bonds suffered right along with stocks.

In the opening months of 1969, stock prices tumbled again, for the reason that, as in 1966, the Fed was making money scarcer and contributing toward higher rental costs for the green stuff by helping interest rates rise. The result was a drop in bond prices timed right on the button with the decrease in stock valuations.

Although investors once had a reliable bond index in the stock market, that is gone. What can they—and you—do now to spot trend changes among bonds?

Crystal gazers are an unreliable group, and bird-watching, while fun for some, has gone out of forecasting fashion since the days of the Roman augurs. The entrails of sacrificial sheep don't tell very much, and few sheep are sacrificed in these cynical days. Tarot cards, palm reading, and tea leaves have gaps in their records. Astrology has scoffers along with its believers.

That leaves us—where?

It should lead us back to the *cause* of increases in bond prices and in the prices of common stocks as well. Back to the money market.

The manager of this market is the Federal Reserve Board, which likes sometimes to pretend that the market runs itself and that the manager only follows dictates of the mechanism. But 't ain't so. The Fed is a strong boss.

Its task is to steer the United States between the Scylla of inflation and the Charybdis of deflation-caused unemployment. The record in this respect is not perfect. But it is a startlingly good one. There are a variety of tools the Fed employs, including on occasions the jawbones of its members who make speeches to talk things up or talk things down, hoping that if they warn that a paddling will come unless naughtiness ceases, that naughtiness will cease (and often it does). But the Fed has at its disposal stronger measures than talk. Principally, it modifies, expands, or contracts the money supply. It can also directly influence going interest rates through its ability to raise or lower the discount rate. This is the interest rate bankers pay when they borrow money from the Fed. Another tool of the Fed is so-called "open market purchases." It also sets the rate of required bank reserves.

If its desire is to expand money, the Federal Reserve buys treasury bonds in the open market. Say it buys $500 million from a dealer known as Simon Simple. Simon delivers the bonds, and in payment the Fed credits Si's bank with the amount of $500 million. The bank, in turn, credits the account of Simple and Co. A quick $500 million has been pumped into the economy because the bank has new reserves on which it can lend.

When the Fed contracts money supply, it sells its bonds, collects back from the economic stream the money which it had earlier manufactured to pump into the stream, and banks' lending ability (*their* ability to manufacture money) has been cramped.

The Fed might also choose to increase banks' required reserves. This means that a bigger portion of deposits must be kept on the books, not loaned out. By such means a more direct method of money control is exercised.

There are other ways to change money supply. But these are the chief tools.

All of them affect bond prices. If money supply should be

contracted the chances are that when borrowers queue up for bucks and find that there are fewer bucks in bankers' hands to satisfy the demand, interest rates will rise. Rates might also rise as a direct result of banks having to pay a higher discount rate to the Fed system.

When this goes on, new bond issues come out with higher interest rates because the issuers will not be able to sell without bigger coupons; borrowers have to offer a better rate to entice investors' money than they did when prevailing interest rates were smaller. That brings about the second effect. Existing older bonds, many carrying relatively low rates by comparison with the new high interest, must adjust to the changed conditions. They then sink in price. When that occurs, the same interest rate figured at par becomes a higher one when figured at the new cost. For example, a 3 percent bond at par would yield 3 percent. But reduce it in price to 60 and its yield becomes 5 percent.

These things have been made the subject of a whole new school of economics. Its leader is Dr. Milton Friedman of the University of Chicago, and his followers have come to be known as the Chicago School. Raw statistics for money supply study are available from many sources. The *U.S. Financial Data* and *Monetary Trends* mailings of the Federal Reserve Bank of St. Louis present them in easy-to-assimilate form. These may be had by writing the Research Department of the St. Louis bank at Post Office Box 442, St. Louis, Missouri 63166.

There are two basic statistics. One is called "money supply." This is defined as money plus time deposits. It is an extremely sensitive indicator which gives a quick current reading. The other is termed "monetary base." This, according to *U.S. Financial Data,* "strongly influences the growth trend of money over periods of several months."

As a speculator seeking leveraged plays in bonds, your yardstick must also include interest rates. Are they historically high? Getting higher? Peaking and about to turn down?

Interest rate levels can be measured in the prime rate big borrowers pay and by the Fed's discount rate. Changes in both are widely covered in the financial press.

You need to know not only whether money rental rates are high, but whether they appear to be going higher. If they are going higher, chances for a quick turn in bond prices that can bring about worthwhile profits with application of the proper leverage are about as slim as a popsicle stick turned sideways. If you buy bonds under such conditions, your leverage pole is going to bounce *you* out of the Road to Wealth.

From observation of the Federal Reserve's actions over the last few decades it would appear that the Fed is a consistent critter. When it begins to move in one direction, it generally keeps going on the new path. It seldom turns immediately back in the first direction.

Putting this observation to practical use would mean buying bonds when, after a prolonged period of increasingly expensive money conditions typified by high and rising interest rates, the Fed takes the first move in the opposite direction by lessening the discount rate banks pay to get new money. It might, after continuingly increasing required bank reserves, let these slack off a bit. It might begin to expand the monetary base or money supply after a period during which it had throttled their growth down to no speed at all. The hint might come in the form of a lowering of prime rate. While prime rate changes come more often than not in the wake of changes in discount rate, they have been known to precede the official rate changes.

When one of these things occurs—*and only when it occurs at a time of abnormally high interest during which there have been successive hikes in discount rate of the Federal Reserve system and prime rate raises by the big banks*—you have a hint that the time to begin a bond play might well be at hand. Should there be an increase in the rate of money stock growth or growth in monetary base *which comes after a prolonged period of either contraction or no growth at all,* your alert to begin collecting bonds has been received.

There is another test an investor can apply—timing study by use of a chart.

Chart experts in the securities markets make a big thing out of their specialty, but it is not so exotic or hard to grasp as some of them would have you believe. If you want all of the tricks the chartists use, I suggest you obtain an earlier book of mine called *How to Chart Your Way to Stock Market Profits* (Parker Publishing Co., 1966).

For bonds, you will need only one chart. The famous Dow-Jones Industrial Average has a companion yardstick called the Dow-Jones 40-Bond Average. It is a good measuring rod of bond market conditions. The *Wall Street Journal* and most bigger community financial sections carry its figures.

You can keep a chart of the D-J Bond Average on either a weekly or daily basis, or—this is probably best—you can read a chart in your public library or your broker's office if either subscribes to a service which charts the bond average. Here is how I explain basic chart reading in an earlier book, *How to Make Money with Mutual Funds* (McGraw-Hill, 1969):

> Sometimes the line which delineates price action on a chart has been bump-bump-bumping against the same upper level without being able to break through to any worthwhile degree. Then it suddenly zooms out of the "resistance area" where price advances had hitherto stopped. When that occurs, the chartist has received a signal, not infallible but probable, that the industry [in our case, bond average] is likely to be in for a rise in months to come. This is called "breaking a resistance line." The opposite of this kind of action, penetration of a lower level from which prices had frequently rallied without having gone below the line, is called "breaking support" and warns the chart watcher that prospects for prices may be growing dim.
>
> On other occasions, an average will wobble back and forth within a so-called "trading range" for months. Now and then it

does so for years. A trading range of this kind can have more or less horizontal lines marking its top and bottom; at other times the boundaries will consist of slanting lines which converge. Technical analysts have different terms by which to describe the two breeds of sidewise action, but when a chart pattern breaks out above or below lines which bound its trading range, the significance is the same whatever the shape of the trading range. The downward break signifies probably sadder days for investors who hold on. The upward break tells an investor that the industry [let's read "bond market" instead of industry] may be in for good times.

These are not the only kinds of chart signals. But if you watch for the simpler signs of changing times and speculative atmospheres, you will be clued in on most of the important new moves. Chart reading is not infallible. It does not foretell the future in any way. It does indicate important trends out of which future conditions can be expected to grow. Charting is another tool to place in your kit. It can help put the bond odds in your favor.

Let's say you have studied all of these things and pored over a chart of the Dow-Jones Bond Average. The signs say "Go!"

Which bond do you buy?

Treasuries? Municipals? Semi-governments? Corporates? Debentures; mortgage bonds; bonds of high, medium, or low quality; convertibles, straight bonds—what?

Below are ten questions. If you answer them carefully, you might find that your choice of which bond to buy, and whether you should buy one or a package, has popped out of the page of scratch paper on which you are marking your answers and that these answers will have made your decision.

Q. *What kind of bond?*

Each type of debtor has something to offer the investors who buy his bonds. Treasuries are ultrasafe. But they are likely to give you slightly lower yield than corporates. As we will see shortly, the amount of incoming interest has to be carefully considered lest the interest going out to a bank which furnishes leverage muscle for your bond play costs so much that you cannot carry on the play long enough to win. Reread descriptions of the bond types. Decide not only on the basis of how much interest but also of what sort of bond fits your needs best. Tax status should be considered. A municipal bond might return lesser yield, but interest you receive from the bonds is tax-free while the outgoing interest you must pay the lender is a tax-deductible item. That consideration matters more to those in high tax brackets than to those who pay a lower percentage on April 15.

Q. *What grade of bond do you want?*

As we have seen, lower bond grades pay bigger yields. They also entail larger risks. Yet the fact is that your bond play is not going to be staged over years but months. Thus the risks over the immediate future when the bond will be held are the ones to be evaluated, not risks which might not materialize until long years away. Keep in mind when looking at the safety angle that "security" behind a bond in reality counts for almost nothing over the short run when you'll be a bond holder. The unsupported note of a good corporation is worth more than the mortagage-backed instrument of a shaky firm.

Q. *A listed or over-the-counter bond?*

Like stocks, some bonds are traded on exchanges, some in the vast over-the-counter market. With a listed bond you can watch price movements more closely. Another advantage is the willingness of banks to lend a higher percentage of purchase cost on a listed than an unlisted security in most cases. An exception would be Treasury notes and bonds which are always traded over-the-counter, yet will nearly always be given the highest loan valuation by a bank. The matter of listed versus unlisted bonds is not an important one, but it should be considered.

Q. *High coupon or low coupon?*

Some bonds are bearer instruments which carry no holder's name. These have coupons which are detached on interest dates and presented, through a bank, for payment by depositing the coupons like cash. Today an increasing number of bonds are registered in holders' names, as are stocks.

"Coupon" rates refer to the rates paid *at par*. Thus a low coupon bond might be one with a 3 percent set rate even though it sells around 60 instead of at par of 100 and returns 5 percent on cost.

This question means: Should you buy a low coupon bond selling at discount or a high coupon bond selling around par? There are advantages to each course. The high coupon bond will generally give you a better yield than a low coupon discount bond of the same type and quality grade. But it seldom offers the same enhancement possibilities. It is easier for a discounted bond to rise toward par than for a high coupon bond to get too far above it. The reason is that when it is above par the bond carries a built-in capital loss if held to maturity, while the low coupon bond below par carries a built-in capital gain for the investor or institution holding it until payoff date.

So since the name of this game is gains, not yield, most players of the bond bit plump for the low coupon bond selling at a discount.

Q. *Diversify or put all the eggs into one bond basket?*

Proponents of both courses are able to make out good cases. I lean to putting all the eggs into one bond basket because bonds are not like stocks. Type for type and quality for quality, they tend to move together in response to the winds that move money rates rather than to the winds of corporate change and the fortunes of industry groups. Diversification becomes unnecessary and merely adds to trouble without increasing safety or making the investment a whit more attractive.

Q. *A faraway or close-in maturity?*

The advantage of a close-in maturity is that if the bond is selling at a price sufficiently lower than par, you are guaranteed a gain. Even though money market and bond price conditions might not work out as you had expected them to, you can wait for maturity and cash up your bond at full par. Your profit is locked in.

On the other hand, you will be competing pricewise with some smart birds who will also be aware of this advantage and whose orders, along with yours, might push up that close maturity bond so close to par that all you will make is interest. But if a bond with such locked-in gain is available, the locked-in feature might compensate for other disadvantages of the particular bond.

Q. *Is there a call clause?*

Such a clause permits the issuer to call in a bond for redemption before the date when it matures. Call clauses are inserted into bond deals for a number of reasons. The chief one is that they permit an issuer to get rid of his high interest debt during times of easier money. Sometimes a call date is so far away that for your shorter-term trading purposes it might as well not exist. Sometimes it is an advantage, because should the bond be called (provided it is a low coupon bond at discount from par) your profit would be immediately achieved. Consider the angles of a call clause if one exists. Most times they won't be important to a seeker after speedy gains. But it pays to know this detail.

Q. *Bearer or registered bond?*

Should you lose a coupon bond with no registration in the street while you're carrying it from your broker's to the bank where it will be put for loan security, you have probably lost the bond for good. It is like cash. Sometimes you will have a choice whether to get a bearer instrument or a registered one in the same security. I advise the registered bond.

Q. *Has my lender a preference for certain bonds?*

Most bond loans will be made with a bank. Banks do not like to find themselves holding too much of one kind of security for the same reason you would hesitate to have a big inventory of cocoa, were you a chocolate manufacturer, lest prices drop and you find yourself stuck. Before choosing the bond to buy, it might pay to talk to Friendly Banker Joe about what collateral he prefers to lend on this week.

Q. *Straight bond or convertible?*

There is the obvious angle of convertibility into common and whether you want to have a double deal going for you in which a common rise can make the bond rise with it in addition to the bond's advantages as a money market item.

But there is another angle also. It applies only to the leveraging of bonds. Once you buy a convert, you will be able to borrow only what the Federal Reserve has at the moment prescribed as margin for convertibles. If you buy the straight bond, the sky and Friendly Banker Joe's willingness to lend his long green are the only limits.

Your tasks in setting up a profitable bond play do not end, although they are nearly over, with the decision as to timing of money market conditions and with the choice of a bond to buy. Banks charge interest, and one matter you must settle with Friendly Banker Joe is how much you will pay. On it may depend how long you will be able to sit out the development of conditions you expect to come to pass. The interest percentage will be based upon the going conditions of the time. At a time ideal for this play in bonds the going rate is likely to be high.

A reasonable rate, in view of the fact that you are borrowing on impeccable security, might be ½ percent over prime.

When prime rate was 7 percent in the summer of 1969, a man might consider himself fairly, even favorably, treated if asked to pay 8 percent even though 8 percent seemed usury a few years earlier.

If you are a favored customer of the bank and in addition offer the top collateral of good-grade bonds, ask for ¼ percent over prime. If you are one of the bank's really good customers, you'll get prime. If they name ¾ percent over prime, things are getting a bit high, and if they want 1 percent over it becomes time to shop a couple of other banks to see whether better terms might be had. Never make the mistake of believing that bankers' offers are standardized any more than competing automobile dealers all selling the same make of car with the same features and fixtures will ask the same price for it.

Interest you pay the bank affects the success of your bond play. You want to be able to wash it out with the interest you receive from the bonds so that you carry your bond package at no cost and are thus able to wait patiently for the coming of the events you foresee. You can wash out the bank interest with your bond interest even though, as will probably happen, you pay a bigger rate of interest than you receive. Here is an example:

Buy $10,000 worth of bonds at current market price. Bonds pay 6½%
figured on purchase cost.

Borrow 80% of cost of bonds	$8,000
Pay bank 8% interest	640
Receive 6½% interest on $10,000	650
Net *incoming* interest despite high bank charge	$ 10

Beware of a situation in which the bank expects you to keep what it calls a "compensating balance." This means that part of the money it lends you must be kept in your account instead of being used to buy and leverage bonds. If you must keep 20 percent compensating balance idle in the bank you are able to effectively use one-fifth less. Moreover, your true interest rate becomes considerably higher as you must pay on the portion tied up in idleness in the account. Not all banks ask for compensating balances.

TO RECAP:

1. Bonds are for widows, orphans—and swingers. They have the advantage of extremely high leverage so that if an investor has properly appraised money market and bond market conditions, a move of only 20 percent in bond price might produce a 100 percent profit on invested capital in very short time.

2. All bonds are I O U's but are not otherwise alike. Treasuries are issued by the United States government. Others are semi-governments such as the bonds of the Federal National Mortgage Association or the Federal Land Bank. Some are obligations of states, cities, counties, and public authorities; collectively these are called "municipals" and are exempt from federal and some state taxation. The largest group of bonds are issued by corporations.

3. Prices of bonds vary three ways—by types described above, by the quality groupings into which they fall, and most of all by variations in money market conditions of scarcity or plentitude of money supply and ease or tightness of interest rates. These, in turn, are generally the result of inflationary-deflationary pressures and of money supply contraction and expansion.

4. Bond investors have fared badly over the long term. But over a shorter term they have frequently seen good gains accrue. It is those short-term gains which offer a Road to Wealth.

5. During earlier market cycles, bond prices moved counter to stock prices. But in recent years, with the same money conditions and fears often affecting both, they have tended to move together. It is therefore a mistake now to use bonds as a

vehicle when stock prices are bearish unless money market study convinces you that the bonds are going to move out on their own.

6. Monetary study should embrace going interest rates in the form of prime rate and Federal Reserve discount rate. It should also take in money supply growth or contraction.

7. Bond market readiness to turn up following a lengthy decline can be studied via charts. The Dow-Jones 40-Bond Average is a companion yardstick to the famous Dow-Jones Industrial Average and is ideal for this purpose.

8. An investor should shop banks for favorable interest. A good rate for the average investor might be ½ percent above the current prime rate in New York City.

9. Incoming interest on the whole bond holding should wash out outgoing interest paid the bank on the borrowed portion.

4
Making It with Mutual Funds

GEORGE WAS puzzled.

He pushed a sheet of paper to his friend Ronald.

"Look at that performance last year," he said, pointing to a list of mutual funds. "107 percent profit one fund added in just twelve months. I could make it even better by using leverage on the fund shares. But almost no fund ever repeats as the top performer. If I had some way of knowing which mutuals might be among this year's top performers, even if I got only the fifth-best instead of number one, I could turn mutual funds into a Road to Wealth."

Can George find such funds? Can you?

This chapter will partly review the material in *How to Make Money with Mutual Funds*. That book covered all of

the kinds of mutual funds there are, including those designed
to produce steady income for widows, orphans, and "prudent
men." This chapter will concentrate upon the kinds of funds
that interest George. It will further look into the ways to push
their results still higher by applying the leverage tool with
which most fortunes today are built.

Mutual funds are poolings of capital in which a number of
investors put their money. The investors receive shares of the
fund, not the portfolio corporations. The fund, in turn, buys a
big assortment of stocks which are the collective property of
all its shareowners. The fund also hires professional management to choose its stocks and to decide when they should be
bought and sold. The advantage of funds to an investor consists in the professional management which, probabilities are,
he could not have hired for himself and diversification among a
wide number of stocks which he could not have achieved unless
his personal capital ran well into seven figures.

A few years ago, the U.S. Securities and Exchange Commission commissioned the famed Wharton School to do a study
on mutual funds. There had been considerable criticism of
funds at the time and one United States Senator went so far as
to claim that by blindly picking stocks by means of a pin
stuck into a board, he had theoretically achieved results equal
to those received from mutual funds. The Wharton School's
study took a lengthy time. Although they did not stick pins
into boards, the researchers came to substantially the same
conclusion as the Senator whose remarks had earlier set Wall
Street on its ear. Funds, the Wharton School reported, sported
stodgy and pedestrian records.

The Wharton School should make a new study today. They
would not recognize the once-plodding old mutual fund industry. In addition to the safe, staid kinds of funds which
were about all the industry had to offer at the time the Wharton research was done, there have been many new kinds which

use all kinds of tricks, angles, and methods to do their thing, which is—performance.

Some funds' performances have been almost as spectacular as the moon trips of the astronauts.

The mutual fund industry's offerings come in many packages. Not all of the packages are suitable for a swinger like George. There are the older funds all of which, although terminology of their prospectuses differs in stating individual objectives, set out to get for their shareowners a certain amount of income, and most of which are hoped to bring home some capital gains too, although with most that is only a side object.

Such funds won't take you or George far along the Road to Wealth.

But there are other funds which zoom along that road. These sometimes blow a tire and go spinning off into the ditch with attendant loss of capital to their shareholders. Such is a penalty of speed. As a group, these mutuals, lumped together by Wall Streeters as "go-go funds," can furnish worthwhile—even rewarding—ways to travel the wealth road.

Some of Wall Street's most sophisticated speculators use go-go mutual funds today instead of buying individual stocks. One of these men explained his philosophy of mutual fund speculation:

"It is an increasingly complicated world," he said.

> A man cannot be an expert in everything. He cannot even be an expert in all of the things which pertain to securities trading. At research into overall market conditions I'm pretty good. So like the traveler who chooses when and where to go but leaves the driving to Greyhound, I prefer to do my own thing and leave the rest of the driving to other people who are themselves specialists. If I am interested in growth in other countries than the United States, the selection of stocks there is best done by a man whose specialty it is. If I want go-go growth in Stateside stocks, I am better off having the choice of

which stocks made by people who do nothing all day but seek and study such companies.

Mutual fund people swing tens and hundreds of millions. They have access to information I frequently couldn't beg or buy. Their analysts travel the country calling upon corporations. Special services of computerized information retrieval are at their disposal; I could not afford to buy the computer time and certainly could not afford to program information constantly into the computers.

This system can be called two-tier management. I furnish the tier of choosing when to go into the stock market. Mutual fund managers furnish the tier of what stocks to buy and when the stocks should be dumped in order to get into newer and more inviting situations.

Results of a system like my friend's can be impressive. Here is the arithmetic of market timing as applied to mutual funds during the troubled, difficult-to-diagnose year of 1968 when so many individual investors, and even a few mutual fund managers, found forward progress almost impossible along the wealth road:

One large go-go fund had a net asset value per share (all assets at current market price, less liabilities, divided by the number of shares outstanding) of $9.98 as 1968 opened. The asset value had grown only to $10.67 by the last week of December, a mini-gain of 6.9 percent. An investor in income securities might have achieved as much.

After President Lyndon Johnson's famous spring speech in which he proposèd the opening of peace talks to end the killing and expense of Vietnam, the stock market went soaring. Many market timing experts regarded the speech as a clear buy signal. If George, our theoretical investor, had purchased then rather than blindly at the beginning of the year, he would have purchased this fund's shares at $8.89. If he had sold at the market top in early December, he would have realized $11.47 for his shares to up the mini-profit of blind holding to a more respectable 29.1 percent gain.

Leverage at 80 percent margin (buying 125 shares instead of 100 for $889) would have increased this gain to 61.5 percent.

One of the dual funds, possessed of internal leverage which we will discuss shortly, had $15.16 asset value at the start of 1968. This had risen to $17.62 by the year's end. The full year gain to an investor who simply bought and held would have been 16.3 percent.

George could have bought at $11.11 after the peace speech. If he had then sold at the December top, he would have realized a net asset value per share of $19.10. The gain: 72 percent. If he added regular loan value leverage to that amount, his gain would have soared to 115.0 percent.

A third fund had achieved the distinction of leading the whole mutual pack in gains during an earlier year. Its gain was not as spectacular in 1968, but was still impressive. At the beginning of January, net asset value per share was $8.71, and by year-end this had grown to $11.95. Gain came to 37.1 percent. Immediately following the Presidential peace speech, the fund's value was $7.65. By the December top in stock prices, it had appreciated to $12.42 for a 62 percent gain. An application of the leverage pole here would have upped the gain still more, to 103.0 percent. (In this fund alone of the three examples, a "loading charge" of 8¾ percent would have been added to purchase price and would therefore have penalized profits accordingly. More on loading charges later.)

An investor interested in fast profit via funds should look for certain kinds of funds and avoid other types. Those which might furnish a fast vehicle for a quick trip along the wealth road include:

■ *Trading funds* which swing big blocks of stock in an effort to stay in the fast-moving stocks only as long as they continue to go up sharply, and then to desert them in favor of some new swinger when they lose upward momentum. When successful this kind of activity makes for an explosively profitable fund. The top-performing fund of a recent year followed this policy.

■ *Long-term growth funds.* In contrast to the frenzied effort to be in anything moving quickly, these funds seek growing situations at what they consider to be reasonable price-earnings ratios and then wait patiently for the situations to ripen. Gains are looked for in years not in months. The second-best performer of the same recent year followed such a strategy. You must make certain this kind of fund produces results and does not merely furnish a home for unwanted waifs of Wall Street whose real growth became stunted long ago.

■ *Funds in specific industries* are wonderful funds to be in as long as their industries continue to prosper and have not fallen out of investors' often-fickle favor. While insurance stocks were darlings of the market a few years ago, insurance stock funds rewarded their holders handsomely. Fund shareowners did not fare as well when the Street's sun ceased to shine on life stocks. Similar examples could be made for many specialized kinds of funds. The lesson is to stay with them as long as you feel—and can back that feeling up with some economic homework—that the industry can continue to do well and its stocks stay on an upward path. Desert such a fund the moment the shade of investment disfavor begins to creep over it.

■ *Hedge funds* are a Wall Street invention to allow profitable speculation whether the stock market moves up or down. They can sell short as well as buy stocks. This allows them to take advantage of any kind of investing climate. Ably managed hedge funds come up with sparkling profits during years which prove disastrous to other investors. What matters is the fund managers' ability to produce as well as promise such profits; you should study what they have accomplished during difficult times of the past to see whether they can do the same thing next year and the year after.

■ *Leveraged funds* have their own internal leverage. They can buy warrants, Puts and Calls, margin convertibles, borrow money here and there, and do all of the other tricks which result, when done well, in heightened performance. Such a fund presents you with the opportunity to add your own leverage atop built-in leverage of the fund. Leveraged funds come in many varieties, colors, and sizes which we will examine more closely as you read further in this chapter.

■ *Funds dedicated to new directions.* "What is Uncle Sam planning to do next?" is a good question to ask yourself in seeking new directions mutual funds. When he was first reaching into space, funds heavy in electronics and missile stocks fared well. When he began to mount a war on poverty, funds with stocks of companies that catered to newly awakened human needs were the thing to hold. But new directions change into old dead-end paths with suddenness. In May, 1969, there emerged from SEC registration a new mutual fund dedicated to investment in conglomerate stocks. At the time of its formation, conglomerates looked to many like corporate winners of the future, and their stocks were high fliers on both the American and Big Boards. By the time the fund emerged, conglomerates were under fire from several sections of the federal government. Many had met defeat in attempts to continue conglomerating. The profits of quite a few were sharply down. The conglomerate form may indeed work out to be a wave of the future, but to the disillusioned investors in spring, 1969, they—and any fund heavy in their stocks—were losers.

■ *Funds interested in emerging ideas.* Trying to spot which of several tiny paths will grow into tomorrow's new directions is a hazardous business. But some funds have done it with success, and their stockholders have become wealthier people as a result.

■ *Resource-participation funds* are not, strictly speaking, mutual funds; rather they are limited partnerships. The resource in which their investors participate is usually oil, the Texas tea from which so many great fortunes have been made. Funds offer investors diversification so that the drilling of one duster won't wreck all their hopes. They also make available skilled geological and petroleum engineering talent. Most of all, they offer a hope and a tax angle. The hope is that dream of many Americans, an oil fortune of one's own. The tax angle is the ability to write off a great deal of the drilling cost directly from income the first year. Sometimes as much as 80 percent of the original investment becomes an instant tax deduction. Then the income from the participation, when things work out as expected, is subject to 22 percent depletion so that a hefty hunk of that is not subject to taxation. Finally, if sold later on, the participation profit becomes a capital gain and taxable as such. (Some tax features are under attack in Congress and could be changed when you read this.)

■ *Mortgage funds* are the red meat of many swingers. They possess considerable internal leverage. Some of a fund's mortgages will be of highest quality, but many will be chosen for high yield. Mortgages generally bring in a higher interest than straight bank loans, and so the mortgage funds possess leverage of the spread between what they must pay to get funds and the interest they achieve on the funds so obtained.

In general the aim of a fund, and the success its management has achieved in bulls-eying that aim, are more important than the particular type. All of the fund groups above offer possibilities for large capital gain. But not all funds within any group bring off the thing they try to do. Their common denominator, regardless of technique, is a search for situations that will go up. Beware certain other types of funds. A wealth-seeker like George should avoid these:

■ *The income funds* are great for old ladies and wonderful for the purpose of anyone who wants to increase the dollars he receives for immediate spending each quarter. But they bring about slow growth, if any. Even when you plow back and compound all of the income received, you are not likely to match results of a fund actively seeking fast movers.

■ *Balanced funds* follow an old-fashioned investing concept of balancing the risks in common stocks with "safer" bonds. There are times to buy bonds; we have looked at those in the Chapter Three. At such times, George and you are better off with the kind of bond purchase advocated there. Performance of balanced portfolios in recent years has been mediocre at best. These are not vehicles likely to whisk you swiftly down the Road to Wealth.

■ *Funds too large to grow quickly.* A slowing of per share asset growth has been the fate of many of the swingingest funds when they reached large size. A portfolio of $300 million and more cannot buy little fast-moving stocks because its sizable orders can't be filled except in older blue-chip stocks. The result in most cases has been that portfolios have diversified into unmanageably different issues or else stagnated in older growth issues of yesterdecade which are still in the account because they cannot be dumped without driving the market down. Many financial analysts say that any fund with over $300 million in assets is too large. Others look for funds under $100 million because of their ability to move nimbly.

■ *An industry fund* when the prospects for the industry are bleak or when, even though companies in it continue to prosper, Wall Street's favor has shifted to new areas of glamour.

■ *A geographical fund* whose area is stagnating or where foreign governments take anti-American attitudes which can inhibit the fund's ability to invest for best results.

■ *Any fund* whose management, despite favorable publicity, smooth talk, and apparent promise, has failed to come up with a good record of results.

Most corporations have a set number of shares. Once sold to the public, those shares trade from investor to investor rather than being sold or bought by the issuing corporation. Closed-end funds are like ordinary corporations in this respect, and that is how they obtained their name. The buying and selling "ends" are closed. Closed-end funds for the most part trade on the New York Stock Exchange along with the stocks of Ameri-

can Telephone, Standard Oil (New Jersey), or Groovy Whiz
Electronics.

An open-end is different. It buys from investors who want
to sell, and it sells to investors who wish to buy. On any typical day an open-end might redeem 25,000 shares and sell
50,000.

Frequently, closed-end shares trade at discounts from their
per share net asset values. This gives an investor extra leverage
because few lights stay long under bushel baskets on the Wall
Street beat, and if a fund is indeed faring well and gives promise of continuing to do so, knowledgeable investors will note
the fact. Their buying is then likely to push the shares of the
favored closed-end back up to asset value. Frequently such
shares go to premiums over asset value. If George had correctly foreseen the boom in Japanese stocks early in 1968, he
might have bought the shares of Japan Fund, an ably managed closed-end traded on the Big Board, at a discount from
asset value. The asset value of Japan Fund soared in 1968 as
its portfolio followed the fortunes of the fastest-growing economy in the world. But the *price* of Japan Fund did even better. It came from a discount under asset value up to, then over
asset value, and was selling at a premium by year-end. The leverage of this discount helped to propel profits for investors in
the popular fund.

Most open-end funds sell at a price which is based upon per
share asset value. But most add a "loading charge"
commission. Loading charge is a reverse leverage pole; it acts
to reduce gains.

Loading charges begin around 8¾ percent. As the size of
purchases mounts, the percentage charge gets smaller. Usually,
investors have to buy in lots of $25,000 or over to get a reduc-
tion at all.

But not all of the open-end funds assess this front-end commission charge. Thus there is another division among funds
into "loads" and "no-loads" as well as open- and closed-ends.

The no-loads are seldom available from dealers since, deprived of the opportunity to earn commission, they understandably prefer to push the shares of a fund which can provide something toward their daily bread, butter, and bourbon. Investors buy no-loads direct from fund headquarters or from a bank designated by each fund as transfer agent.

While it is desirable to avoid the penalizing load charge, that charge should not be the *only* factor in a decision on whether to buy or avoid a fund. If a load fund can produce superior results, it frequently gives investors a better run for their money. When fund shares are held over many years, the loading charge becomes an ever-smaller factor since it is assessed but once, while the fund, if it is a real go-go, goes on making steady profits over the years.

In *How to Make Money with Mutual Funds* I suggested some yardstick measurements to use in determining a mutual fund likely to furnish upside performance. Let's review them here.

One is to watch the growth in per share net asset value. But be aware of a gimmick that sometimes affects this growth and, many financial analysts say, makes growth seem bigger than it truly is. This gimmick is "letter stock," unregistered with the Securities and Exchange Commission and bought on a letter of investment intent stating that the stock is to be held a certain time before being registered and sold. Often letter stock is purchased at a considerable discount from the price of free stock. In one or two cases, funds have marked up letter stock almost to the value of the free stock. (Say a company's free stock trades at 20. Mutual Fund A buys a block of letter stock at 13. If it then immediately carries the letter stock on its books at 20 it has created instant performance. Yet it still holds something for which there is no market for a long time to come.)

But few funds buy letter stock at all, and those which do are more likely to follow more realistic policy. The manager of one high-flying fund wrote to his shareholders regarding a holding of letter stock:

"The stock was purchased at a discount of approximately 30 percent from market value at the date of agreement. The stock is currently priced on our books at a 30 percent discount from market and the discount will be held at this level until the stock becomes fully registered."

You can apply five tests of per share asset growth to decide whether you are buying a fund likely to make big gains for you:

Q. *What is the five-year compounded average annual asset growth?*

To obtain this, add back the capital gains distributions over each of the years to current net asset value per share, divide resulting figure by the net asset value of five years ago, and look at the five-year compound interest table. Example:

Fund's asset value per share now	$18.90
Capital gains distributions over 5-year period	1.10
Total	$20.00
Asset value per share five years ago	10.00
Divide $20 by $10, and the result becomes	2.0
Refer to table whose nearest com-interest to 2.0 is 2.01, and you get compounded average annual growth of	15.0%

Some funds have sudden good years after a series of bad ones. Laggards and losers for five years, the funds specializing in insurance stocks were suddenly big winners in 1968 because of the return of insurance stocks to investor favor. Later when this resurgent interest flagged, insurance funds again became the plodders that they had been for half a decade.

Q. *What is asset growth during the past twelve months?*

Sometimes fund managers' magic touch fails under changing conditions. A check on latest performance will help you to keep your venture capital out of palsied hands.

FIVE-YEAR COMPOUND INTEREST TABLE
(1 plus i)^n

Percentage	Amount	Percentage	Amount	Percentage	Amount
1.0	1.05	15.0	2.01	33.0	4.16
1.5	1.08	16.0	2.11	34.0	4.32
2.0	1.10	17.0	2.20	35.0	4.49
2.5	1.13	18.0	2.29	36.0	4.66
3.0	1.16	19.0	2.39	37.0	4.82
3.5	1.18	20.0	2.50	38.0	5.00
4.0	1.22	21.0	2.60	39.0	5.28
4.5	1.25	22.0	2.70	40.0	5.37
5.0	1.28	23.0	2.81	41.0	5.55
6.0	1.34	24.0	2.93	42.0	5.75
7.0	1.40	25.0	3.06	43.0	5.97
8.0	1.47	26.0	3.17	44.0	6.19
9.0	1.54	27.0	3.30	45.0	6.41
10.0	1.61	28.0	3.44	46.0	6.64
11.0	1.68	29.0	3.57	47.0	6.87
12.0	1.76	30.0	3.71	48.0	7.10
13.0	1.84	31.0	3.86	49.0	7.33
14.0	1.95	32.0	4.00	50.0	7.59

Q. *And during six months past?*

This gives an even quicker picture of whether the fund is performing.

You can also apply momentum tests to a number of mutual funds. When one of them begins to falter, and its push-ahead power drops to less that that of stocks in general you want to get out and seek instead a fund likely to appreciate faster.

"But George," his broker said to him when he switched funds for the third time in eight months (each time at a sizable profit), "mutuals are meant to be bought and held. Let their professional managers do the switching. You hold on."

"Phooey," George replied. "I want my money run up, not sideways. This fund's professional is stubbing his toes too often. See how momentum relative to the overall market has slowed down. Maybe he is stuck with a lot of 'out' stocks. No reason why I should also be stuck with them. Switch it, buster, switch it."

Here is how George calculated momentum of mutual fund asset growth:

■ Each week, he noted the percentage rise in a half-dozen fast-moving funds kept under surveillance. This was done by subtracting the last week's net asset value from this week's and considering the difference as a percentage of the previous week's figure. Loss percentage was calculated in the same manner but in reverse, subtracting this week's figure from last week's and again considering the loss as a percentage of the previous week's asset value.

■ Then he made an identical computation for the New York Stock Exchange index. "You can use any market average you like," he explained to the broker. "I like the NYSE index because it is an average of all stocks. But the Dow-Jones Industrials, Standard and Poor's 500, or Barron's 50-Stock Average would do if you like one of those better. The idea is to use *something* representing 'the market' for a comparison with my funds' performances."

■ If his fund did better by either appreciating more in a week when the market went up or going down a lesser percentage during a down week for the market, then George smiled and marked the fund "plus." If it did worse than the market he gave it a "minus." A with-the-market performance rated "even."

■ George next constructed an index. He began with the round number 100. Each week a mutual fund beat the market, he added in its plus to move the index number higher. If the fund lagged behind stocks, in general, he dropped the index number by one. If Fund A had three pluses, two minuses, and another plus in as many weeks, the index would look like this:

100
101

102
103
102
101
102

■ When after weeks of steady rise the momentum index drops, but not lower than the last level it reached on a drop, George figures the fund still has strength relatively greater than the market and stays with it. But if it declines below the level of an earlier drop, he quickly trots his shares from bank box to broker's office, sells them, and switches into a faster-moving fund.

"I'm measuring the fund manager's ability to stay in up stocks," George explained. "When his assets aren't growing as well as the overall market, then he is holding the wrong stocks."

George paused a minute.

"Now let's look at some late data on *dual* funds," he told the broker. "I like their leverage. I can get over 100 percent of other people's money working for me in duals."

Dual funds have two parts. Half of the investors own income shares. The remainder own capital shares. To the first group goes all of the income generated by the whole fund. Buying 50 percent of the fund, the income investors receive 100 percent of the dividends. The other half of the fund belongs to the capital investors and they, too, get 100 percent of the fund working for them.

Moreover, as fund investors hungry for capital growth, the second group often benefits from added leverage of a closed-end discount. We have seen how this works in the earlier case of Japan Fund. After their introduction in 1967, the duals became closed-ends.

If a dual fund's portfolio should appreciate in net asset value by only 15 percent a year—several did this during the troubled year of 1968 when so many other go-go funds fell on their performance faces—then net asset per share gain applicable to the capital investors would not be 15 percent but 30 percent. Such a fund might have traded at the beginning of the year at a discount from asset value of 18 percent and seen that discount narrow to 8 percent during the year. This happens when closed-end funds such as the duals are performing well. Now assume that George were to buy 100 shares worth $10 per share in asset value at the 18 percent discount, paying $820 for them.

Add 30 percent appreciation to the asset value, and the shares would be worth $13 per share if the fund were broken up.

At the year-end discount of 8 percent, the shares were trading on the New York Stock Exchange at $11.96. In practice, no listed stock could trade at such a figure since price movements go by eighths of a dollar, so round this off to $12.

George sells.

He has invested $820 and realized $1,200 for a profit of $308 or 34.5 percent *while the underlying value of the whole portfolio went up only 15 percent.*

Not being content with the double leverage of the dual fund setup and the discount from asset value, which he correctly expected to narrow or vanish during the year due to recognition of successful fund growth, George added a third level of leverage by purchasing on 80 percent margin.

Then the numbers game went like this:

*Investment of $892 purchased 125
shares rather than 100*

Sell 125 shares at $12	$1,500
Gain after sale	608
Percentage gain	68%

Utilizing three tiers of leverage, George had parlayed a 15 percent growth in the fund's portfolio value into a 68 percent profit for himself.

"At such a rate," he said to Ronald that evening, "a man can double his money in a year and a quarter according to the compound interest tables!"

Dual funds are not the only ones possessed of internal leverage to which outside leverage can be added to produce a springy pole capable of making capital values truly jump and zoom. Some funds are designed to use the tricks described in Chapter Two on stock trading. They buy warrants, Puts and Calls, own convertibles, and use all the borrowed money leverage that law and Federal Reserve regulations allow.

On top of that, George and you can add the additional leverage of margin of your own. Since mutual funds are almost by definition poolings of capital invested in common stocks, the Fed rules which set common stock margin rates also govern the amount of money your bank or broker can lend on the security of fund shares. The rate is at present (and expected to continue) the same as set for common stocks.

Utilizing 80 percent margin instead of 100 percent ownership may not appear to be great leverage. But all of the profits made on extra shares it is possible to buy because of margin go (if you prove correct and fund indeed appreciates in price) into pure net profit which can make you a wealthier man in no great number of years.

Some have the internal leverage of senior securities. Leverage of this type works with funds as it does with stocks described in the chapter regarding corporations' internal leverage. After senior security (bond or preferred stock) income and sinking fund requirements have been met, nearly 100 percent of the extra results accrue directly to the fund's shareowners.

A volatile fund portfolio affords still another kind of leverage. When investment people talk about volatile stocks they mean big swingers which might move up 10 percent to 15 percent on an active day and which, alas, are also subject to big downward swings on the days when things do not go well. A volatile portfolio jumps when the market rises a polite 1 percent. With added outside leverage from margin, such performance can be exaggerated into tremendous gains.

TO RECAP:

1. Mutual funds are poolings of capital which afford individual investors diversification and professional management. There are nearly as many varieties of funds as there are of common stocks.

2. Today, many sophisticated traders and speculators trade with mutual funds. They depend upon fund management to furnish the first tier of stock selection. Since many funds are too big to get completely or even mostly out of stocks when the market dips, they depend upon personal judgment to furnish the second management tier of selling out altogether when the conditions are not propitious for appreciation of the stocks a fund holds. By such tactics, the results from simply buying and holding mutuals can be considerably improved.

3. Certain kinds of funds can afford a spirited ride on the Road to Wealth. Others plod slowly under even the sunniest economic skies. It pays to know which vehicle can whisk you along at a fast clip.

4. Open-end funds buy from investors who want to cash up and sell to others wishing to buy their shares. Their capitalizations are open at both ends. The funds with set capitalizations are called "closed-ends." Investors buy from and sell closed-end shares to other investors.

5. "Load" open-ends tack on a commission as high as 8¾ percent to the net asset value of their shares. "No-load" funds sell at asset value and are usually redeemed the same way.

6. Speculative swingers like George measure a fund by growth in per share asset value. If a fund can bring about 15 percent average growth year in and year out for five years, its management has displayed agility under many different kinds

of conditions. Judgments should be made also on both long-term and intermediate-range asset growth.

7. Funds' momentum can be calculated to compare growth in asset value with growth or decline in the overall stock market. When fund action relative to all stocks begins to stagnate, it is often time to switch to another fund more attuned to current conditions.

8. Some funds have built-in leverage of their own to which the outside leverage of margin can be added.

5

How to Cook Profits from Raw Land

In my home city of New Orleans vast tracts of swampland and the gunk and semiswamp that Louisianians call "trembling prairie" lay for decades below the limits of the city proper. The area was called New Orleans East and most people considered it fit only for breeding crawfish and a few alligators. It had been within ownership of the same families for generations.

But a man named James J. Coleman saw possibilities. Lawyer, bank chairman, highly successful businessman, Jimmie Coleman had a vision of what those trembling prairies of New Orleans East might become if properly developed.

He interested powerful Texas money people in his project. At the time this chapter is being written, New Orleans East has become prime residential property. The swamps have been filled. On them, houses have been built. Streets have been laid out. Utilities reach New Orleans East and the section has all of the city services enjoyed by New Orleans' oldest sections.

Jimmie Coleman did something for that land that all of its ancient owners had not done. He saw a *use* for it. And he made it conform to his vision of usability.

Therein lies the key to vast profits in raw land. Envision a use. If you cannot envision usefulness for the land, don't buy it. There must be a reason why land will appreciate in value —or it won't appreciate, but rather lie stagnant and almost valueless.

You need not have the millions needed to drain swamps, put in utilities, lay out streets, and hire salesmen. But you do have to see a use, however far in the future, and a way whereby through development the land might triple, quadruple, quintuple in value. Such a goal should be always in mind.

Then if you apply the leverage pole, you have opened up a vastly profitable Road to Wealth through finding, valuing, and exploiting raw land.

In 1967, the U.S. Department of Housing and Urban Development issued a study made by Grace Milgram and Christine Mansfield of the HUD staff. It was called *The City Expands* and covered changes in land usage and values from 1945 to 1962 in the city of Philadelphia. Particular attention centered on the conversion of land from rural to urban use.

"The development which has taken place has been accompanied by an increase in average price per acre," they wrote.

Expressed in current dollars, there has been a 13-fold increase in the 18 years, from $1,030 per acre in 1945 to $13,300 per acre in 1962. In deflated dollars, the increase has been seven-fold, from $1,350 to $10,250. The price of residential land has risen only slightly less, from $1,400 to $10,100 in deflated dollars, an annual rate of 14.5 percent. This increase indicates the market response to two major types of forces, those cross-sectional factors associated with varying characteristics of the land, such as improvements in accessibility and shifts to denser zoning classes; and those factors associated with increased population, employment opportunities in the area, and other measures of general economic and demographic growth which has taken place over time.

This is a mouth-watering history of profits, especially when considered against a background of the leverage which Philadelphia land owners may have used while values were thus increasing. But it is, alas, a history, and history, while it sometimes repeats, cannot be depended upon to do so. Some people say right now that the peaks of land values have been passed. They contend that the big money has already been made by the Jimmie Colemans of yesterday, leaving little for you and George to skim off tomorrow.

This is a sobering thought.

In 1945, financial worriers announced that land prices were leveling off. By 1950, they were certain that there was no more growth to be had in raw land values. (Real estate people use the term "raw land" to mean undeveloped acreage on which—as one wit once quipped—the hand of man has not yet trod.) In 1955, they were convinced that only doom awaited speculators foolish enough to invest in raw land with the hope of seeing it appreciate. By 1960, tired of watching others make millions out of opportunities they were sure did not exist, the pessimists knew that by *then* land's opportunities had all been wrung out. 1965 saw land values still higher, and the doomsayers were still preaching that the world of big money from land was surely coming to an end.

That world has not ended.

Some people are sure today that the opportunities are really and truly and cross-my-heart-hope-to-die over at last.

Are these people finally right?

They are not. Raw land is still a Road to Wealth.

It has to be so as long as populations all over the world continue to expand, and as long as the affluence of those populations continues to increase. People's expectations and realizations of better living are going up even faster than their numbers. Well-established trends like this almost guarantee that raw land, rightly chosen and wisely sold, will prove highly profitable in years to come. Perhaps even much more so than in the years which are past.

In a recent speech, U.S. Secretary of the Interior Walter J. Hickel said: "About 70 percent of the people of the U.S. live on 1 percent of the land. Each year, three million more Americans are being shoehorned into cities that are already filled. It won't be long until 80 percent are living on 1½ percent of the land."

Writing in the magazine, *Buildings,* S. N. Tideman, Jr., President of the Society of Industrial Realtors, said regarding another land use:

> Industry generally has taken its new establishments away from the congestion of the central city, preferring suburban or rural locations. New highways—particularly the Interstate system—have spurred this trend. Suburban or rural locations offer large sites to accommodate modern, one-story plants, plentiful space for parking and expansion, generally less expensive land and labor costs, lower taxes, and improved employee morale through pleasant working conditions.

Large corporations with the staffs, computer time, and specialized skills to get informed views about what might come in future are enthusiastic about land ownership for still other reasons. Said George H. Weyerhaeuser, President and chief executive officer of Weyerhaeuser Company:

"Our nation is faced with a shrinking forest land base, a population explosion and urban sprawl. . . . There must be full public understanding that most material wealth comes from the land in one form or another."

Del E. Webb, Chairman of the Board of Del E. Webb

Corp., indicated in his 1968 annual report that long-range land development on a sizable scale had just been undertaken. Webb's faith in the future of land values is strong.

Another factor is the drive to eliminate urban blight from our society and to furnish all of our citizens with decent living conditions. This assures new needs and uses for land in the years to come. We will look into this in greater detail in another chapter. Meanwhile, it is important to consider and understand the background factors and facts which brought about appreciation in raw land values and which promise to bring about even greater appreciation in years to come.

Interested in all of this, our friend George recently took a university course in demographic trends. The word "demographic" comes from the ancient Greek word for people, *demos*, and it refers to the movements, aims, trends, aspirations, actions, hopes, and fears that people everywhere have and that shape their actions. Many of the actions being shaped have a direct reaction and effect upon land usage, for land is the thing on which all of us live. Deprived of it, people have no place to pitch their roofs, no ground in which to grow their crops or on which to graze their cattle, no sources of minerals, or places on which to build their factories and plants. Without land mankind would be dead.

Man's uses for land determine its values, George learned. "Hence," he told Ronald, "it is man I need to study, then apply his trends and wants to land."

George's demographic studies led him to certain conclusions:

■ *"Man has more disposable money, over and above what he needs to live,"* George pointed out to Ronald. "This is even true in the least prosperous of the underdeveloped and the developing nations. Compared to the fully developed lands, these seem poor. But compared to what they have been throughout history, they are rich indeed. And the developed, advanced countries are also enjoying affluence such as no one even ten years ago would have dreamed of. It all brings about certain results."

One of the results is money to spend on leisure time activities. A decade ago, Disneyland in Anaheim, California was one of the wonders of the world, reachable by only a fraction of the population. That same area, expanded, entertains many times the visitors it did ten years ago. Shortly, Disney Corp.'s Florida park will open. Between the two are many parks like them: "Six Flags over Texas" in Dallas, "Astroworld" in Houston, "Six Flags over Georgia" in Atlanta, and others. The increased affluence of people make these possible. The superparks' land use extends far beyond their immediate areas since to support them there must be new motels and hotels, new eating facilities, and new parking areas.

The same affluence is felt in increased land usage in towns far from facilities such as Disneyland. People can eat out more often. There are more good restaurants in every city now and a proliferation in medium- to low-price eateries featuring fried chicken, hamburgers, roast beef sandwiches, and the like. (More of this particular trend in a later chapter on franchising.) The key thing about all of this as it regards land is its effect in creating new needs and uses for land, much of which was idle and cheap a few short years ago.

The trend, George concluded, is more likely to accelerate than to slow down in the years ahead of us.

■ *Man is pushing out to the suburbs.* Tired of squeezing together into old buildings, weary of being what Interior Secretary Hickel called "shoehorned" into cities that are already filled, people today are reaching out to the sprawling suburbs which were once the exclusive sign of largest cities such as New York, Chicago, and Los Angeles, but which mark every city of any size today.

In these suburbs, people have room to breathe. Often they live in detached, single dwellings which take more land than the upward-reaching apartments of the city centers. (These latter are by no means dying, however; the need for them is increasing and will be dealt with in a later chapter.)

I talked not long ago to a veteran real estate man. "Land I believed would never be used for anything except growing weeds has become prime residential property in the last few years," he told me. "And the trend is increasing. I wouldn't be surprised to see land on the moon going at high prices by the time my children reach my age."

■ *The moves of people bring about new shopping patterns.* Grandfathers of today's merchants looked around for an inner-city location when they wanted to build a store. They purchased just enough for the building itself to stand upon and there, crowded together like soldiers on a parade ground, stood the big stores of yesterday. The stores of today are different.

The most noticeable thing about them is their freer use of —and need for—land. The stores are likely to be of one- or two-story construction because people no longer want to visit departments layered on top of each other like the parts of a gigantic steel and concrete cake. They want to stroll leisurely about. And so the stores go out instead of up. To do this, they need land.

Moreover, they are surrounded by acres of what yesterday's retailers would have regarded as waste space. Paved and carefully painted into lanes, these serve as parking areas. Shoppers will no longer go to a store which does not offer ready access from car door to store door. Parking areas take awesome amounts of land. It has been remarked by one city planner that before long most of America may be covered with concrete in the form of roads and parking lots.

The trend here, too, looks as if it is moving faster, not slowing down.

■ *Swifter transportation is spreading people out.* Once a man had to live a short streetcar ride from his work in order not to spend the day going to and fro. Then the automobile allowed him to move out to the city fringes, then to the suburbs. Now with freeways and expressways as crowded as city streets, the trend is to mass rapid transit. It is probable that when the drag of war costs is finally removed from the budget, a great deal of United States spending may be for the 125-mile-per-hour trains such as that which is presently whisking people about the New York-to-Philadelphia megalopolis.

■ *Yet the inner city areas grow too.* Many of our city centers have become blighted by overcrowding. Crash programs are in the talk stages and in some cases have already been implemented to give even the poorest better quarters in which to live. "Humane people would be shocked if a zoo kept animals as some of the very poor live in our inner cities," said a prominent sociologist. "Something *must* be done about it. Soon."

Happily, something is being done. What is happening opens avenues for people like George to perform important social services and at the same time earn merited gains of the type that, with leverage, can quickly build fortunes. More about this in following chapters.

■ *The vanishing of the very poor.* Today, industry is attempting to train and rehabilitate people formerly considered unemployable, whom society had once discarded on the trashheap as useless. Governmental plans are going into effect to educate and remotivate people who had never in their lives had training, some of whom could not read or write, nearly all of whom lacked the will to try because there was no place for them to do their trying.

The results to date have been slim. Programs of this type can only work slowly, and some experts say it may take a whole generation before anything begins to show. But, concluded George, in the almost certain abolition of poverty in developed parts of the world, and abatement of its worst effects in the less-developed areas, lay assurance that land needs must increase astronomically over the years to come.

■ *Development of totally new cities.* These will be planned to meet all of man's needs and will not be allowed to develop helter-skelter as so many of our older cities have done. They will include areas for recreation which are lacking in present cities. Their educational and cultural facilities, like those for housing and recreation, will require the use of much land still today in a raw condition. Inside such planned communities are likely to be plants, offices, stores, all of the facilities furnishing work and supply for inhabitants.

These are largely in planning stage. A few are under development. All share one requirement: They will add high value to land not presently devoted to high-value usage.

■ *People are buying second homes,* and it is not only the very wealthy able to own posh summer quarters who do this.

The home used for weekends, possibly for vacations, and at all times as something to look forward to as a relaxant, is not always a fancy place with luxuries or a swimming pool, although homes of even the middle-middle class have these features now. Swank or stripped to basics, a second home occupies *land.* The trend toward second homes is pushing up the values of waterfront acreage everywhere that there is a lake, gulf, bay, seacoast, or just a clear, pretty stream on which to perch a weekend home.

Rural property, too, is going up as a result of the trend— which appears to be strong although just beginning—to ownership of retreats outside the crowded cities and away from suburbs which are themselves coming to seem packed.

If the trend becomes tidal, it will increase land values in areas where second homes are placed because of the need for golf courses, community swimming facilities, new eating establishments, supermarkets, drug stores, and other fringe services needed to cater to part-time dwellers.

■ *There will probably be a speeded-up wave of new births* which in turn will bring about new needs.

Twenty-five years ago, people accustomed to the curtailed birth rates of the depression years spoke in wonder about what they termed the big baby crop which followed World War II when 13 million servicemen returned home to marry and beget families. Now that big baby crop has grown up and is having its own babies.

"Consider," said one population expert, "how land usage suddenly spread out as people needed more quarters, more services, more of everything largely as a result of the high birth rates of 1945–1949. That population surge changed the face of the nation and made raw land worth many times its wartime cost, sometimes scores of times its depression price. Such a thing could happen again. It may be starting right now."

From his demographic studies, George learned that there is one key to success in appraising, buying, and holding raw land, then selling it for a profit. "That key is *value added*," he told his wife. "You don't have to add that value yourself, although there may be more profit in it if you do. But you have to see how it might be added, then go out and—if you're not going to do it yourself—find someone who will buy the land at a profit because of the idea you have given him. The *idea* can be the added value."

"Simmer down, George," Sophie replied. "What is this bit that has you so excited?"

"It's like this," George answered. "Take a piece of raw land ten miles out in the country. The area I have in mind is adjacent to the river. As corn land it is not particularly rich and could probably be had for a song. The question is: What value can be added to the property while it is in my hands which will make it worth more to another purchaser?"

He popped the top off a bottle Sophie had produced from the refrigerator, slipped off his shoes, and poured a head on the glass of beer.

"Now let's look from another viewpoint. As farming land, it is just so-so. It is not on any important highway. But it is very close to the main street of the little town that is nearby, and that main street leads to the Interstate highway. In one direction, the Interstate goes west. In the other it goes right into the downtown heart of the city. A most interesting fact.

"Suppose—let's just suppose—that a big tourist attraction could be built on such land. How many tourists have ever seen the mighty Mississippi? They have read of it in Mark Twain's books. They have seen pictures of it. Many people coming this way might like to live a few days beside 'Ole Man River.'

"See where I'm driving? Now let us suppose a bit futher. Suppose someone could get his hands on that land, fill it in where it needs filling, level its hummocks and high spots, grade it, landscape it, and then rent out parcels of the land to big corporations. One corporation might put a national-name motel astride its parcel, another a restaurant, a third a gift shop. Is the picture beginning to emerge? *Value is being added to the land.* The owner could stipulate certain minimum standards of construction and service. He could put into his leases provision for a percentage of sales and/or profits from each of the establishments to whom he rents land. Why, that farmland could be one of the richest parts of the city if value were added to it!"

Such addition of value need not take the form of actual grading, parceling out, building, selling, and/or leasing. *The mere addition of the idea could add sufficient value.* George pointed this out:

"The value is there right now. Accessibility to the Interstate highway via the adjacent main street is the key to the whole thing. It would permit travelers to stay in this Mark Twain land development and still, when they wished, drive in minutes into the heart of the city for shopping or sightseeing or theaters or anything else they wanted that a big city provides."

The idea of such value addition took hold in George's mind. Next morning, he approached a real estate agent. "See how much they'll want for an option to buy that farmland," he said. "Let the option be at a specified price I approve, and let it hold for six months. Make sure that I control at least 500 feet of land for a half mile fronting on the river."

The farmer-owner was delighted to have an offer for land he considered marginal and from which very little of his income came. After slight haggling, the agreement was signed giving George option to buy within six months at a figure close to the one he had determined in advance. The agreement stipulated that, should he buy, the option fee would be accepted in downpayment.

"Now my problem is whether to develop it myself or trying to bring in outside financing to help me," he told Sophie that night. "I believe I can get enough leverage into this thing to swing it if I try. But if I do I may be missing out on some important expertise that others could furnish. The best thing probably is to play it for a raw land deal and not try to be developer, too. I've added enough value with the *idea*."

"Have you the capital to do even that?" asked Sophie.

"Easy," George replied. "All I'll need is the amount I put up to obtain the option. Watch me leverage the rest."

Much of his eventual profit, George was aware, would depend upon arrangements that he made now. Option fee of $5,000 proved to be his total eventual investment other than operating expenditures. George now did advance work with mortgage people and with the seller.

He had expected interest rates to be high. "But not as high," he confided to Sophie, "as they proved to be. I'll be paying over 8 percent. But it is worth it, for I don't expect to need the money very long. And I have a commitment from a mortgage company so that I can obtain 60 percent of the eventual purchase price of $100,000 the minute I ask."

Next, George approached the prospective seller. Aware of his eagerness to fob off for $100,000 a piece of land which was not producing $2,000 in crops annually, George was able to persuade the farmer-owner to take back a second mortgage on the land. This was in the amount of $43,500, also at 8 percent. Now he had a financial base from which to work.

He next commissioned a local artist to prepare sketches of

the land as it would be when the value he envisioned had been fully added to it. The sketches showed rolling riverfront dotted with the forms of motels, restaurants, shops, and other resort facilities. These were put together in a brochure which explained the idea. Total cost: about $500.

Copies of the brochure were sent to business development managers of eleven motel chains and restaurant firms. No firm commitments were asked for. Several chains indicated that they would look at the development carefully.

Armed with other copies of his brochure, he went to see a real estate firm which represented important investment money from corporations interested in land values.

"See," he said, "what a long-term profitable resort can be built here. And here (he flung photocopies of letters from motel chains onto the desk) are resort firms seriously interested in participation."

Out of dozens of conversations came a valid nibble. The client was a conglomerate corporation. Agreement was reached to sell the land for a price of $195,000.

Since George was selling the land, not the option, he exercised his option to buy, arranged for his loans to be transferable to the purchaser with the purchaser having an option of assuming the two mortgages or paying them off.

Act of sale and title search took some months.

At the end of the time, George was able to total his results. They went like this:

Investment in option	$ 5,000.00
Direct expenses	500.00
Interest costs, 3 months at 8%	2,533.33
Total investment and costs	$ 8,033.33
Receipts above amount of mortgages	100,000.00
Net profit after investment and costs	$91,966.67

"That's a 1,115 percent return in only nine months," said George to the accountant whose task it was to figure income taxes. "Ideas bring big returns when you apply them to the value added concept of speculating in raw land."

As George correctly noted, the length of time it takes a deal of this sort to come to fruition affects its desirability. If the deal had taken nine years instead of nine months to work out, interest charges might have eaten away a considerable portion of the profit. And taxes continue whether the land is sold or not.

A deal expected to work out in one year, then, is not as good a deal if it works out in three, four, or five years.

In this example, George sold the land after adding the important value concept of a new usage for land then having only minimum-value usage. In later chapters we will examine the potentials that can exist if George or you add physical value instead of simply selling a concept.

The range of usability concepts for undeveloped land is very wide.

Has it potential for a shopping center? For such potential to exist, there must already be some residential buildup of land close by. Roads capable of carrying heavy traffic must be in existence or at least in the plans stage. Some notion of buying patterns must be formulated along with a decision as to whether those patterns are capable of being changed by a new shopping facility.

Are office needs in the area big enough for a new building? A survey of this could include potential as well as actual need. Many corporations are shifting from crowded central business districts into areas where employees can find parking.

Is the property near water? Waterfront properties, even in rural areas, are coming to have tremendous value. The growing leisure people enjoy today leads them often to where swimming, boating, and fishing can pass the time. Some developers near but not adjacent to water have brought the water to their properties by means of canals and artificial lakes, making the backyard of every home site a private marina.

Has the land usability for manufacturing? Many manufacturers, particularly in light industry, are moving out to and often beyond the suburbs. In appraising and selling land for this kind of use, you can often obtain invaluable help from industrial development boards. Every state has a department, and sometimes a special commission, devoted to bringing in industry. Cities and counties have people whose jobs it is to sell industry. Electric and gas utilities often set up staffs to bring new users into the territory. These people have active files of prospects and needs. They can advise you about the planning of new utility lines around which plant site development can be started.

In the mid- and late sixties big corporations began to take an interest in land developments. Among them were Westinghouse Electric, which has an Urban Systems Development Department, and Alcan Aluminum, with its Universal Homes division.

Would a model town do well here? Self-contained communities will be hungry users of raw land as our social needs force revision of the old urban patterns.

In looking at new land sites, it is necessary to view them not as parcels of dirt, cropland, or weed patches, but as the possible buyer will see them. If your concept is residential, your customer—unless you choose to be developer as well as land merchant—will be a builder-developer. In the U.S. Department of Housing and Urban Development study mentioned earlier, *The City Expands,* it was pointed out (taking the developer's viewpoint) that:

> Among sites on the market, the choice is limited by the topography and drainage, including assessment of the possibility or cost of changing contours or eliminating any other obstructive features or, alternatively, of being able to utilize the scenic opportunities as a marketing aid. Next, consideration must be

given to the existence of community facilities, the zoning, the possibility of having streets and utilities laid by the city, the general character of the surrounding neighborhood and of the roads by means of which major groups of customers must approach the site.

Recently, the Federal Reserve Bank of St. Louis made a study—"Growth—Metropolitan vs. Nonmetropolitan Areas in the Central Mississippi Valley." Reporting on this in its *Monthly Review* of January, 1969, bank statisticians wrote:

> Several basic national trends have probably contributed to the emphasis on metropolitan areas. The number of people living in metropolitan areas rose from 94 million in 1950 to 132 million in 1966. In contrast, the population in the farm sector dropped sharply. The number of people living on farms declined from 23 million to 10 million, and the farm portion of total population declined from 15 per cent to 5 per cent. This large flow of people from farm to city has intensified problems of transportation, air pollution, crime, housing, and education. Because of the great interest in these problems and their association with larger cities, it is often assumed that metropolitan areas are growing more rapidly than other sectors.
>
> In contrast to the above assumption, this article indicates that metropolitan areas in the Central Mississippi Valley (CMV) states (that, is, Arkansas, Kentucky, Mississippi, Missouri, and Tennessee) have not been growing faster than nonfarm communities outside metropolitan areas. Smaller cities, towns, and urban-type communities in this region (excluding the farm sector) have been growing at substantially faster rates than the large centers, according to such measures of economic activity as population, employment, and wage payments. Furthermore, total bank deposits and per capita personal income have been growing faster in nonmetropolitan areas (including the farm sector) than in the metropolitan centers.

Some people who live in cities and never see land that is not paved nevertheless find profit in the stocks of companies that buy, sell, build upon, rent, and wheel and deal with land. These range from corporations owning oil lands, which may be all or partly under lease to operating companies, to firms using their land for cattle grazing and include the big outfits that erect and operate multiuse structures. There are also real estate investment trusts and other companies specializing in adding value to land.

Land offers financial leverage. But this leverage won't do you much good—indeed, it may do you considerable harm— if you miscalculate or if you pay too much for land so that what you pay approximates what you are likely to get.

There are two basic kinds of loans made on real estate. The first is interim financing and the other long-term loans. If George had wanted to put up motels and hotels on his riverfront land, he would have secured interim financing to swing the acquisition of the land and to pay start-up costs, etc. As the buildings progressed, he would have drawn increasing amounts of long-term loan money to replace interim. Since George optioned and then bought the land without adding physical values himself, his need was for relatively short-term money.

Longer-term loans are made by conventional lenders like the savings and loan societies, insurance companies, and the mortgage firms which are often their local agents. Mortgage loans on raw land are likely to be shorter-term. Banks make these as well as the conventional real estate lending agencies. It is well to consider some things before making any loan.

1. *The Interest* Local conditions affect this since borrowing for mortgages, institutional as well as home, often tends to be made by hometown institutions at hometown rates. Always remember the differences between interest and discount. If you pay simple interest, you will pay a straight amount on your mortgage to reduce principal and a varying amount that represents the interest, which goes down as principal reduces. Many mortgages are written so that the borrower pays a fixed amount regularly, with the percentage going into interest and that into principal reduction varying over the length of the contract period. In general, it is true that you reduce your principal (and hence the amount of interest) faster in the first half of the mortgage term by the first method.

A discounted note is one in which interest is tacked onto the front end of the principal amount borrowed and then payments made to retire both. Under such a plan (more common with chattel than real estate loans) the interest is assessed for the full period of the loan even though the principal on average is about half the amount borrowed.

2. *Do You Have the Best Interest Rate?* When you buy an automobile, taking along for trade-in your two-year old station wagon, you might find great variance in the amounts dealers quote even though they quote on the same purchase with the same trade. One dealer might have his used car lot full; he would have to wholesale any car he took in trade. Another might be in need of cars to sell secondhand. It is the same with lenders. One might have his money coffer full and be seeking mortgage borrowers the week you apply, another could be loaned to the hilt. It therefore pays to investigate more than one money source and to shop for terms as you would on any other purchase.

One way to achieve lower interest is to assume an existing older mortgage should you buy land or buildings which the seller does not own outright. Chances are that he negotiated his loan in a time when rates were lower than now.

In any event, your mortgage, to be a favorable one, should contain two clauses. The first is one permitting the borrower to renegotiate interest rates should the prime rate charged in New York go down by, for example, a point or more. Sometimes such clauses contain automatic provision for reduction of mortgage interest by one point for every point reduction in prime rate. Or the clause might be pegged to the Federal Reserve's rediscount rate. A change-of-interest clause can be very important under today's high interest conditions.

The other clause a very well-negotiated mortgage should contain allows a borrower to prepay principal amounts. Often there is stipulation as to the minimum amount the lender will receive, and sometimes such payments can only be made at set times as, for example, each anniversary of the mortgage contract. Often the clause permits prepayment only in multiples of a set number.

3. *A Next Consideration Is the Land's Loan Potential* "Different types of lenders are only allowed to make certain kinds of loans," a corporate treasurer wise in the ways of borrowing explained to me.

> Each will make a package that is the best he can in view of his restrictions and of the amount of lendable funds he has on hand at the moment. Unless a borrower knows all the avenues and lengths of mortgage, acceptable collateral, etc., on which lenders figure, it can pay him to look at three or four different *kinds* of mortgage loan sources—a bank, perhaps, then a savings and loan institution, an insurance company, even a factor.

Achieving a property's best loan potential can best be done before the mortgage is signed—seldom afterward.

Included among such potential lenders might be the seller of a property. Often sellers are willing to carry part of the notes, and on occasion all of them, in order to cinch a favorable sale. On other occasions the seller might want his payments spread out for tax purposes. Occasionally he will accept a lesser interest rate than other lenders in order to gain in a different direction.

The Housing and Urban Development Department study, *The City Expands,* pointed out another financing method. "Land may be bought on an installment system, under which an agreement of sale is executed for the entire tract but title is taken piece by piece," the authors, Grace Milgram and Christine Mansfield, pointed out.

The arrangement is advantageous to the builder because the price for all the land is set at the time of the agreement. Interest is scheduled, but no adjustment is usually made for possible changes in the value of the dollar or of the land. The seller may like it because it provides a stable return and reduces taxes by spreading income over several years.

Real estate investment trusts sometimes use a technique that you might employ if you own a corporation with stock trading publicly, or if you are willing to incorporate with a view of later "going public" (to be discussed more fully in a later chapter). Your stock or convertibles can be used as money for purchasing land. Sometimes it is possible to issue letter stock, discussed in an earlier chapter.

An example of financing via stock rather than money occurred recently when one real estate investment trust—Wall Streeters call them REIT's—arranged to give 142,000 of its shares, which were listed on the American Stock Exchange, in payment for considerable tracts of commercial and industrial property.

Before making any kind of loan commitment, however, the investor who is wise to the ways and the pitfalls of real estate satisfies himself about certain things.

He looks into zoning, for if local laws prohibit a use of the land which he has in mind, talks with lawmakers should establish a firm commitment to change the zoning. Zoning is a touchy subject in many communities. Often investors have come croppers over such restrictions. Many who neglect to negotiate or litigate away zoning problems will continue to lose money, and to them leverage will be a danger, not an advantage of land investment.

No one should need to be warned against "investing" in blue-sky land which cannot be actually seen and walked over. Yet simple people go on buying advertised land half a continent away on the promise that utilities will be put in, and later development will take place. In a sad number of cases

this never comes about. Most of the land developers who operate nationally are honest people selling honest value. But
there are enough fringe operators in blue-sky land to keep in-
vestigatory commissions and the courts busy and the suckers
broke. A consideration often overlooked is availability of clean
water. Without it land has only minimum potential. Writing
in the magazine, *Area Development,* August, 1968, Sheldon S.
Brown pointed out that:

> Sometimes areas with an attractive labor surplus for the es-
> tablishment of factories are unable to provide enough fresh
> water either for use by personnel or for industrial processing.
> Their supply proves inadequate to create steam for turbines
> needed to generate electricity, because water's purity level for
> this purpose must be higher than that ordinarily required for
> human consumption. The former plight of Southern Italy ex-
> emplified this deficiency.
>
> Let's also examine what has been happening in the Baja Cal-
> ifornia area of northwestern Mexico. Peasants from all over the
> country have flocked there in recent years looking for work, but
> have found mostly grief and unemployment. Manufacturers
> couldn't move in until electrical power and clean water were at
> hand—this despite abundant land, a large labor pool and tour-
> ist dollars.

Some land investors travel to the bankruptcy courts because
of a simple lack of title search. Land improperly transferred,
or on whose title a cloud still sits, is not saleable merchandise.
Saving a lawyer's fee here is one of the poorest economies you
can make.

TO RECAP:

1. The key to profits in raw (undeveloped) land is the
value-added concept. This consists of seeing, and sometimes
bringing about, a use for the land which no one has as yet
provided.

2. Sometimes physical value is added by a developer or im-

prover of land. Ways in which this can be done will be studied in greater detail. Sometimes the added value is conceptual —a view of potential land usage or profitability which is sold *along with the land* to the person or company that will later develop and sell improved real estate.

3. A United States government study recently indicated that land values in a typical area appreciated at an annual rate of 14.5 percent. There is no reason to expect this rate to decrease in years to come. There is, in fact, reason to expect that the rate may accelerate.

4. A 14.5 percent annual increase can loom large in a field where considerably less than that amount is required as downpayment to swing financing. Frequently, no immediate cash-in-hand amounts are required at all.

5. A number of demographic, people-oriented factors are behind the trend toward real estate value escalation. These include the push to the suburbs; the growth of new shopping patterns in which branch stores out of central business districts frequently sell more merchandise than the parent stores which are penned up inside inner business areas; swift transportation to speed people farther away from the former hubs of urban existence; the elimination of poverty; the growth of new inner cities; the development of totally different urban concepts; affluence which allows middle-class people to own second homes; a speeded-up wave of new births.

6. The length of time it takes a proposed real estate deal to ripen should be considered along with the projected profit, since profit is desirable or inadequate judged by how much time capital might be tied up.

7. A recent survey in the Mississippi Valley states indicated that faster-than-urban growth of land values is coming about in the small towns.

8. Nor should land potential be viewed only in residential terms. Other uses include industrial, commercial, shopping, and waterfront.

9. Tremendous leverage comes from borrowed money.

Often a second mortgage can be added atop a first, so that only closing and selling costs come directly out of capital.

10. Some mortgages are more advantageous, some more fitted to special buying and selling circumstances than others. Borrowing terms affect later profit.

11. In addition to conventional mortgages, there are a number of other ways to finance land purchases.

12. But before any land is purchased or even considered, such factors as water availability and zoning should be examined. And the securing of a valid, saleable land title is vital to later success of a land venture.

6

Community Improvement — for Profit

THE NEXT PARAGRAPH might put you right in the middle of a wide Road to Wealth. It was written as part of a comprehensive report, *Urban Housing Needs Through the 1980's: an Analysis and Projection.* The report was prepared for the National Commission on Urban Problems by Dr. Frank S. Kristof, a housing economist of note.

"All projections for the decade of the 1970's point to the largest absolute and proportionate increase in households on record," Dr. Kristof wrote.

An increase of 12.3 million households is projected for this decade, and it is expected to result in the greatest sustained output of new construction experienced in the nation's history—an average of 1.98 million units of all kinds annually. *Conversions and other additions are expected to swell this total to 2.1 million added units per year.* [Italics supplied.]

There are two parts to this projected new housing boom. Both or either could be the answer to your wish to be wealthy. The first is embodied in Dr. Kristof's word "conversions." This involves the upgrading of older dwellings to make them habitable. In its most workable form this calls for bringing shabby, dilapidated old structures back to the levels of the neighborhoods in which they sit. Some call it the "repair and resell market."

The second part is truly big. Most of us know it as urban renewal. Big corporations are involved in it, and there are not mere millions but tens and dozens of billions of dollars involved. There is room for an individual—you or George—to get into this movement and to make it b-i-g. Read what another noted expert, Daniel S. Berman of Fink, Weinberger and Levin in New York, wrote in the June, 1968, issue of *Buildings* magazine:

> To the imaginative, aggressive professional, urban renewal offers the opportunity of building a fortune in a single, well-conceived, well-managed project. No other field offers such unique money-making opportunities to management with know-how and persistence.

There is a new movement of people underway. If a time exposure picture of the tides of such movements were possible, you would probably see a broad flood moving out of the cities and into suburban homes that sprawl around the rims of all of our metropolitan areas. You would also see a small stream moving in the opposite direction, back to the metropolis with its teeming streets and clogged inner traffic arteries. Strange as it may seem, the backward river is the one which is increasing in volume. It is still comparable to a little brook and the movement away from the city to a broad, strong river. But the little brook may soon begin to overflow its banks as the movement grows stronger.

Sick of long travel via freeways to work inside the city, weary of the smaller selections often found in suburban stores, frustrated by the tighter zoning which forbids a quick trip around the corner to a drug or food store, people who moved away from the city due to one set of aggravations are beginning to move back because of another set of annoyances.

To George, this back-to-the-city movement made sense. "I'm a city boy," he told Ronald one Saturday afternoon after a heated game of tennis. "Me for the paved sidewalks and the Narrow Open Spaces, consisting of a strip of green between the front door and the street. People who move back to town show sense. I've got it figured how to make a buck out of the trend."

George's angle was not original. "That's why I like it," he added. "Long ago a very rich man gave advice to a young man just starting out in life and anxious to get the word of wisdom from the wise old bird's own mouth. 'Never innovate,' this successful executive told him. 'Leave that to those who want to take 50–50 chances. *You* want to get rich. So wait until you see an idea that has already proved its worth in practice. Try to make sure that it is in an area where the action is just beginning, not in anything like buggy whips or stone axes for fighting saber-toothed tigers. Then go out and copy that idea unashamedly.'

"Not everyone should do what that old rich bird advised. But in this case I am influenced by the fact that the remodel-repair-and-resell bit has proved remarkably successful."

George could have pointed to a number of examples. One executive of my acquaintance who spends his daytime hours five days a week as purchasing agent for a paper company spends his evenings and weekends lovingly fixing up old houses. Once work on one of these has been completed, he and his family move in until another prospective remodeling job comes to his attention. Then he makes plans to sell House A in which he has been living for half a year and move into House B after its remodeling has been completed. Over the years he has lived in a wide variety of houses and made comfortable profits on each transaction.

The homes this executive buys for resale usually come in neighborhoods of the inner city. Such opportunities are found in the smaller towns as well. In the little community of Marrero, Louisiana, real estate operator Sam Menszer has rebuilt over forty rundown dwellings, planted trees and shrubbery, and transformed an area verging upon suburban slum into one of respectable homes. Yards that were once debris-littered became spic and span. "A fellow who lives in a sloppy house gets a sloppy attitude toward his dwelling," Menszer reported. "The same people later take great pride in the appearance of their houses. They even go out and bug their neighbors to spruce up."

While the social benefits of Sam Menszer's activities are great, his basic aim was profit-oriented.

Unless you are going to rebuild the whole neighborhood, as urban renewal plans to do and as Sam Menszer did in a more modest way before the renewal program became a national drive, then you have to look first for a section that is not going down but which contains a few houses which are. Almost always, this defines an older section. It can be in a suburb or in the central city. In newer areas the rundown process that creates a repair and resell bargain has not had time to work.

One man whose whole living—a very good one—comes from this kind of activity concentrates attention upon one old but still high-cost area of his city. Staying inside the limited territory keeps his finger tightly upon pulses of changing community life so that he has become a shrewd judge of potential values within a small world of real estate that is about three miles in length and no more than two miles in depth.

In judging such an older section for yourself, you must ask, as this man does, certain questions:

Has the Section High Marketability?   There are older areas that tend to keep their faces scrubbed and their limbs and bones in good shape because a staid, settled group lives within. But sometimes the look is only superficial. If there is not high marketability, you will do better giving such a section the go-by. Even if your remodeled and repaired opus of carpentry and concrete should turn out as expected, any difficulty in early sale would increase your stake, decrease profits, and reduce the leverage upon which a successful Road to Wealth depends.

One frequent cause of low marketability is that the children who grow up within an area move to newer sections when their families begin to grow up. A large number of older inhabitants, few children at play, and low enrollment in schools of the neighborhood are bad signs. Marketability might be low. The people within meticulously maintain their property, but no new families move in.

Watch the telltale For Sale signs within such an area. If these stay overlong on the houses that are offered, the section has low marketability.

Are Values on the Upgrade?   Marketability isn't enough. You want your section to be one whose values are increasing so that the up trend of the whole area will help to carry your remodeling job to a profitably higher price. In this age of high inflation, which is sometimes checked or slowed but which always seems to burst out anew after a few years, just maintaining the same values is not standing still—it is dropping behind.

Records of real estate transfers are usually public documents. They tell who bought what house, from whom, and for how much. Consult these. Nothing can give you as close a feel of the trend of values as a look at the prices for which houses actually went to new owners. But look at the whole picture. What happens to one or two houses may not be typical at all, and you may have haphazardly chosen instances of forced sale to settle inheritances or spots where other special circumstances such as zoning rules made the values drop. (Sometimes special circumstances make values go up as well as down in a fashion uncharacteristic of the area. I recall an instance of a wealthy family bidding a $30,000 house up to $100,000 because they wanted their married daughter to live around the corner from the old family mansion and didn't give a hoot what they had to offer the stubborn owner to persuade him to sell.)

If you are going to interest yourself seriously in the buy, remodel, and resell bit, the classified section must become required reading every day. Houses do not always (or often) go for the asking prices. But these give an idea of the trends of pricing. From them you can estimate what a remodeled house of similar construction and size on a similar street might be able to bring.

What Is the Trend of Recent Zoning Board Rules?   For repair and resale of residential property you do not want to do so in a section that zoning authorities are beginning to open to commercial or industrial usage. Similarly, if you see the potential for two fine apartments in a house that was ideal for the big families, live-in relatives, and servants by the pair which people had in an earlier, simpler day but which is hardly usable for modern groups, then you have to know the zoning problems you might meet. If it's a one-family street and zoning planners are adamant on keeping it that way, forget your big house. It can only become a loser.

Real estate people say that the trends of zoning rulings are as important to know as the current rulings themselves. When a former one-family street lies among other streets of similar houses which are being zoned multifamily, then you have a chance to persuade the authorities that in your case the alternative to multifamily might be no usage at all.

What Is the State of Repair of Surrounding Structures?   If the neighboring houses are themselves rundown—even if they are only beginning to be so—your chances for this particular repair and resell gambit go glimmering. My friend whose profession is the rebuilding of inner-city property says:

> I take a car window survey. That is, I drive by and examine other houses up and down the street and around the corners. If it appears that they may reach a state of disrepair and peeling paint about the same time my proposed acquisition is spruced up, then the potential house bargain isn't any bargain at all. But I am always impressed when I see work underway at other houses. That indicates that the property which surrounds my proposed acquisition is itself on the upgrade.

Choice of area is important. Choice of the right house is equally so. On the examining, discarding, and bargaining steps that take place here will depend eventual profit or loss.

"Remember," my friend stressed,

> you have to shoot at doubling your money. That does not mean that if you pay $30,000 for a house you must realize $60,000 from it. But if you swing that $30,000 house with a $4,000 downpayment, and if you then put $6,000 into repairs, you should look to realize another $10,000 from it, thus doubling your actual cash outlay.
>
> However, actual cash outlay need not be $6,000 to effect a $6,000 remodeling job. This kind of work, too, can be leveraged. Probably a $1,500 downpayment would be sufficient.
>
> Then if you put $3,000 down, and an additional $1,500 out of pocket to swing a $6,000 remodeling, you would have socked $4,500 into the house. There would also be interest to be paid on both the property loan and the money borrowed for remodeling during the time both loans remained in your hands—call it $500. There would probably be another $500 of incidental

expenses. So you might be $5,500 out of pocket. Then your arithmetic should go like this:

Cost to swing deal on old house	$ 3,000
Downpayment, remodeling loan	1,500
Interest cost expected	500
Anticipated incidental cash costs	500
Total out of pocket	$ 5,500
Profit desired	5,500
Cost of house	30,000
Price for which house should sell	$41,000

Therefore—you must ask yourself: If I put in repairs that I plan to do, will I be able to make this $30,000 house into a $41,000 house? Do similar structures on the street or on surrounding, similar streets bring this kind of price right now?

In the remodel and resell field you will live or die by the accuracy of this kind of potential profit computation.

What Is the Borrowability of the House as It Stands? The computations above demonstrated that size of your downpayment and the rate of interest to go out while the house is in your hands will determine profit or loss on the nice little house with the rundown front, shabby paint, and antiquated plumbing located among all those well-kept upper-middle-class homes on Eagle Street. If you had to place $8,000 instead of $3,000 as initial downpayment, then the eventual selling price needed to make such a deal pay out will increase to $46,000. Possibly you feel after careful consideration that $46,000 is realistic and that you can get it. So go ahead. But *know* what you need. With leverage as our big tool for beefing up the profit, an idea of borrowability becomes vital.

Try to work with only one lender. This might be a savings and loan institute, a mortgage company which represents insurance companies or other investors, even an individual if you happen to know wealthy people who like to sweeten their returns with mortgages yielding more than bank deposits or good bonds. Working with a single firm has advantages. The last time I bought a house, an agent of one such outfit came out and gave it what he called an eyeball estimate of loan potential. This proved to be within a whisker of the loan which was eventually approved.

(Borrowing to finance purchase of an old house itself will probably be done through a savings and loan institution or from a local mortgage lender. Borrowing for improvements can be done from either of these sources or a bank.)

Does the Price Represent Real Undervaluation?   Two years ago, I watched a pro go about evaluating a bargain home. The buyer was an architect schooled in structural values. He lived in the area, an older city section of very good homes, and was aware of buildup possibilities. The seller was an estate whose beneficiaries were anxious to turn the old family property into cash.

"The house was pretty shabby," my architect friend told me when we discussed it one morning.

> No one has lived in it for a couple of years, and no one has kept it up for a lot longer time than that. However, the changes do not need to be structural. A lot can be done with landscaping. Inside the plumbing is so old it has museum value. There are wash basins in the bedrooms that no one wants today. All those old touches will have to go. But again, the thing is structurally sound and what makes me want the house is the asking price: $40,000. Homes right on that block go for twice as much. I would judge that the lot with nothing on it is worth the asking price all by itself.

That was his criterion of a bargain: A house, sound but in need of repair, situated on a lot which, even without the house, appeared to be worth the price.

Is the House Close to Schools, Churches, and Public Transportation?   The advantage of close public facilities is seldom found in an outlying area. It is the reason why many people willingly pay high prices for older central city homes.

Ten years ago, I sold an older home in sound condition but lacking the fresh new woodwork and some of the other touches to be found in a brand new suburban house. People who commented on the woodwork were shown quickly through, thanked, and forgotten. Those who expressed interest in the nearness to schools and churches and who valued the desirable location in an old part of the city received close attention, for those items of proximity and location—not new woodwork—were what I had to sell.

How Close Are the In-city Universities?   "University section" was a valued real estate phrase some years ago. But there appears to be a trend for the big-attendance schools such as universities to deteriorate rather than add value to surrounding property.

Students now come in automobiles and sprawl these cars over the surrounding blocks, since older campuses in the midst of cities seldom have off-street parking for any except a few faculty members. Neighbors find the parking spaces in front of their houses taken away. Students who do not live in dormitories seek rooms or small apartments near the campus, and this, too, lowers real estate values. Crowds brought to football and basketball games are not always considerate of the grass and gardens of the homes where they park their cars.

"Face it," one real estate man told me. "The universities are making areas around them into slums, except for newer campuses, generally on the outskirts of cities, which have on-campus parking and dormitories." Not all experts will support his view, but there are enough examples of college-bred property deterioration to warrant your being leery of property close to a university.

However, *commercial* property usage close to campuses can be inviting, provided the local zoning or planning boards approve your taking the grand old mansion on Eagle Street and putting a restaurant in its basement with apartments above.

How Long Will I Have to Hold Before I Might Find a Buyer? Real estate does not enjoy the liquid market of stocks and bonds. That is why it pays to watch velocity of real estate sales on Eagle Street. If its mansions, however grand, seem to move like frozen honey, then your costs will mount with increasing interest payments and with the invisible factor of lost gains from other deals to which the capital might have been committed while that slow mover on Eagle Street finally becomes a home for something besides your dwindling capital.

Big Changes or Little Changes? "Cosmetic" changes consist of things like paint, refinished flooring, or landscaping which can make a house look like an expensive place without entailing any big expense at all. "Structural" changes may make the place last longer but won't necessarily make it look better. Structural changes can cost so much that they will render the whole project unwise to undertake and unprofitable to finish. Smart repair and resell operators look for houses where they won't have to do much in the way of big-time structural changes. They look for places where the right cosmetic changes can turn an old barn of a place into something a smart, house-wise housewife will look at and say, "Gee, Sam, wouldn't we be comfortable living there."

Some changes involve so much that if the need for them is there, you would do better to get back in your car and drive out of that neighborhood as fast as the law allows. An example is shoring. Where foundations have cracked or sunk, a house has to be jacked up just like an automobile whose tire is being changed and new foundations put in place or reinforcing added to the old. Your bill for shoring only begins with the job itself. Shoring is almost certain to crack some interior walls as the house is lifted and jostled. It puts door frames out of whack, splits ceilings, makes things cease to function, and brings about the need for a host of cosmetic repairs as well as minor structural jobs.

Termite damage can often extend far beyond the little rotted timber you are able to see down at the ground line. If an expert examines it and tells you that the bugs have made themselves a big meal and that the house needs extensive repairs, twist the point back into your favorite ball pen, put on your hat, and depart. Fast. That house is a capital trap.

Nearly any remodeling of an older house will involve plumbing. Where this can be kept to a minimum, go ahead. People who have done this sort of thing warn that it is a good idea to keep plumbing additions close to existing plumbing. If you plan to add a bath, put it atop one which is on a lower floor. Or directly below the upper bathroom, even beside it. Carrying plumbing long distances through an old house can make the bills grow big without adding compensating value to the investment.

Remodeling costs vary from city to city. Even within a city, different contractors quote widely differing prices. The National Bank of Commerce in New Orleans has issued a set of ranges within which a typical repair-remodeling job might fall, with a set of probable monthly payments which would have to be met on a loan. The tables are reproduced here with permission of the Bank. If you use them, remember that at best they are guidelines. The cost estimates are based upon 1969 data.

We Are Sold on Home Improvement, But How About Some Idea of Costs?

Here is a handy chart showing various typical additions, modernizations, repairs, and renewals. Remember, these costs are only estimates, based on local averages of recent jobs. These figures are intended to be guides only.

Job	Price range	Approx. monthly payments *	Explanation
Adding a room	$1,680 to $5,000 or more. Price range from $10 to as high as $25 per sq ft. Average about $18	$110	Price figured on basis of 12- by 14-ft room. Low price figured on pier foundation, sheet rock walls, two windows, one door. High price for deluxe materials including built-ins, picture windows.
Modernizing a bath	$700 to $1,500	$40	Lower cost is replacement of fixtures only. In old houses, plumbing usually must be brought up to city code. This plus ceramic tile adds to expense.
Adding a bath	$1,200 to $2,500	$60	Presumes existing house space is used for new bath. Cost of new plumbing is main difference in adding or remodeling bath.
Remodeling kitchen	$1,500 to $4,500	$100	Middle price would include new appliances, cabinets, floor, wall, and ceiling finish. Deluxe job with breaking out walls runs much higher.
Enclosing a porch	14- by 8-ft porch, with jalousies, from $500 to $1,000. Other methods usually run higher	$25	Adding heat for year-round room makes for middle of price range.

Job	Price range	Approx. monthly payments *	Explanation
Making recreation room in basement	$3,600 to $6,800 for area 20 by 20 ft. Range from $9 to $17 sq ft	$170	Minimum finished ceiling height should be 6 ft 8 in. or better 7 ft. If pipes must be moved or foundation slab broken, cost rises. When excavation is necessary, be sure all sides are waterproofed. Built-ins add to cost.
Converting garage to family room	$1,600 to $3,000	$75	Cost affected by materials used and type of finish favored.
Finishing an attic	$4,200 to $5,600 for room 14 by 20 ft	$160	Includes stairway, strengthening joists, insulation, framing, wall, ceiling, and floor finishing for family room, hobby area, or bedroom. Price varies with size of rooms and materials. Dormer windows add to expense.
Adding single carport	$600 to $2,000	$45	Lowest cost is for flat-roofed construction with sufficient foundation and bracing to withstand high winds. More expensive; built-up roofing, storage cabinets, grillwork trim.
Reroofing	$270 to $400 for average five-room house exclusive of guttering	$10	Price range from 235-lb asphalt shingles to new 20-year bonded type. A few roofs are potentially lower in cost. Most (asbestos-cement, slate, cedar shingles, clay tile) are higher. Number of gables, off-sets, etc. increase cost. Replacing flashing also ups price.

Job	Price range	Approx. monthly payments *	Explanation
Paneling a room	Approximately $300 for 12- by 14-ft room. Add $100 for accoustical ceiling	$10	Price based on panels at $10 each. Wide price range in available panels.
Sheetrock a room	Approximately $450 for 12- by 14-ft room	$15	This is good modernization for old house with cracked plaster walls. Price estimate includes lowered, suspended ceiling, complete finishing of walls and woodwork. Owner could save by doing own painting.
Patio with barbeque	About $750 for area 10 by 20 ft, reinforced	$25	Terrazzo is now popular material for patio. Brick is old favorite. Slate and flag-stones also excellent. Last three materials somewhat more expensive.
Swimming pool	15- by 30-ft pool, from $2,500 to $4,500	$115	Shape of pool, type of coping influence price, as does ad-ditional depth for diving, a diving board, ladder, under-water lights. Basic pool price includes filter, medium-sized patio, all cleaning and main-tenance equipment.
Central heating and air conditioning	About $1,600 to service 1,000 sq ft	$55	Includes equipment of ample capacity, installation and duct work. Often old houses necessitate more expensive duct work.

Job	Price range	Approx. monthly payments *	Explanation
Painting house exterior	Approximately $600 for five-room house. Price range from 12 to 15 cents per sq ft	$20	Number of windows and doors in house influence price. Type of surface preparation needed before painting also consideration. New latex paints slightly more expensive than oil paints.
Adding a fireplace	$750 $1,300	$35	Cheaper to add fireplace on outside wall. Inside installation requires breaking through, patching floor and roof. Height of house also cost factor. Some variation in cost of brick.

* 36 months average—monthly payments for up to 60 months are proportionately less.

It is claimed by some remodel and resell experts that the fastest way to add value to an old house is to modernize its kitchen. The next-best value-adder is to put in more and better baths. The old one-bathroom house is as passé as the Studebaker which flourished at about the time in the late forties that many homes were being constructed with one bath. Those now older homes seldom had worthwhile laundry areas, partly because the appliance stores had none of the modern labor-saving laundry equipment women use today. The addition of an airy, pleasant laundry area can increase a house's value in the eyes of the family member whose decision will most sway the family's purchase or rejection of your remodeled jewel on Eagle Street.

During the forties and fifties, many houses were built with only two bedrooms. The two-bedroom home can only be used by newlyweds or by people whose children have grown up, married, and left, and the latter group is likely to look with a better eye on a home which provides space for children and grandchildren to be house guests. Next on the list of value-adders, therefore, is a new room for the home with what today's householders regard as cramped quarters. Frequently, an existing basement or attic can furnish all of the space you require without having to put a roof on top of, or a foundation below, your expansion.

In older sections of the central cities, even in some of the surrounding suburbs whose lifeline is the freeway and whose raison d'être the automobile, homeseekers frequently find no off-street parking. A driveway and carport—if in conformity to city planning regulations—can considerably enhance the attractiveness of that Eagle Street residence without adding a great deal to the cost of remodeling. Some older houses have garages which probably fitted the narrower cars of a long-gone day. Today, only Junior's Honda will get inside without danger to the bumpers and paintwork. As replacement, a modern carport, styled in conformity with the prevailing neighborhood architecture, can add value along with convenience.

If you like to work with your hands and know how to do it, you can probably save on the costs suggested by the National Bank of Commerce's tabulation. That is an especially good idea if you're a beginner at the remodel and resell game.

Older hands find that it takes a lot longer to do it yourself, even where you have the know-how and tools. That longer time might add enough in unexpectedly higher interest costs to offset the savings of the contractor's profits.

Many entrepreneurs who have been at the game for a long time and have picked up expertise along the way make the plans themselves. But others say that the services of an architect are crucial. "True," said my acquaintance, the purchasing agent and part-time home improver, "an architect gets fees. But he knows a great deal about construction I do not know.

He is familiar with building codes—sometimes they pop new things into the codes, and you don't even know that they are there unless you're a pro. Most of all, a good architect has access to new ideas, new methods, new decorative twists that I would not see. He doesn't cost. He pays."

The contractor and architect can make the house resaleable for you. But they can't sell it. When the time for that comes, you will again have to make the decision whether to do it yourself or hire a professional property peddler. A good deal can be said on both sides of that question.

I recall selling a home which had been cosmetically remodeled some years ago. It was put into the hands of a real estate agent who, in three months, showed the house to three prospects and got a nibble from none. Engrossed in other work, I put the house into the hands of a second professional seller. This one brought me a single offer 25 percent under my asking price and unacceptable.

At the end of the second three-month period, I watched the taxes, insurance, and interest mounting up and took things into my own hands. An exterior photograph was combined with a brief description of the house's salient advantages and a headline was put over all of it: "Remodeled and Reduced!" The asking price was lowered by what would have been an agent's commission. One thousand advertising broadsides were printed.

These were sent in batches to every real estate office, with a notation that full commission would be paid if an agent sold it, but that no contractual listing would be entered into. Two hundred of the broadsides were retained and given to everyone who responded to a small classified advertisement using the same appeal, "Remodeled and Reduced!"

Within a few days after these actions had been taken, some twenty different agents showed the house. Three valid offers were received, none through agents. One was accepted. After the usual time for title search, etc., the house was sold.

On the other hand, there have been a great many instances where amateur efforts such as my own failed flatly, and the professional efforts of a trained real estate agent have succeeded.

So you pays your money and you takes your choice.

Whichever choice you make, it is a wise idea to get loan appraisal. Then when a prospect asks you or your agent what sort of terms can swing the deal, it is possible to say, "The Spiffy Savings and Loan will take X dollars down and make you a twenty-five-year loan at Y dollars per month plus insurance. That is, if you pass their credit requirements."

You won't be likely to have the choice of doing things yourself, however, if you get into the really big end of the remodeling game. This is the activity known as urban rehabilitation. It is going to be one of the sizable factors in our economy in years to come. Many economists say this will have an eventual impact upon America comparable to the permanent impact of the Employment Act of 1946 which put the federal government squarely into economic planning by making the maintenance of full employment and a stable economy Uncle Sam's direct responsibility.

Research Report 9 to the National Commission on Urban problems was prepared by Allen D. Manvel, associate director of the Commission. Writing in regard to urban centers of over 260,000 population, he noted that these

> . . . had 31.2 million housing units, or 53.5 percent of the nation's total housing stock. Three million of these housing units in the largest metropolitan areas, or nearly 20 percent, were found to be "substandard" when that term is defined as "dilapidated" or, although better than this from a general structural standpoint, lacking hot water, running water, or a private toilet or both. More than 2.9 million of the occupied housing units in these were "overcrowded"—i.e., they averaged more than one resident per room.
>
> The poverty areas of the central cities typically have a considerably higher "housing density" than other parts of these cities.

In 1960, the poverty areas had 3,071 housing units per square mile, or 64 percent more than the 1,874 per square mile average for the remainder of the cities. However, the poverty areas also had a higher proportion of vacancies, so that in terms of occupied housing units the disparity was not quite so great— 2,839 per square mile in poverty areas, or 59 percent higher than the 1,787 per square mile elsewhere in these metropolitan cities.

There, then, is the problem—dilapidated, overcrowded dwellings, lacking basic facilities for human beings in the latter part of the twentieth century, yet not profitable either, as evidenced by the vacancies.

Doing something about the problem is not a job you or George can accomplish with a couple of thousand dollars as, more than occasionally, you can succeed in dressing up an old residence in a better neighborhood. Yet the leverage *is* there. Urban renewal might offer more of it than any other potential Road to Wealth. Urban renewal is so big that even a leverage pole of a size which looks little in comparison with the overall job is big in absolute size.

"Where else can I swing a $2 million deal with $50,000?" asked one operator. It is true that leverage of $50,000 to move $2 million is tremendous. But $50,000 remains a lot of money. If you have it, you might consider urban renewal as a way to put it to work in the hope of a fortune as well as the expectation of doing a great deal of ultimate good to your disadvantaged fellow men.

Despite the fact that it is generaled from Washington, urban renewal is essentially a local sort of deal. So it is with local people, local problems, and local officialdom that you will find yourself working.

Typically, the local public agency, whose name might vary from that but which is likely to be known as the LPA, sets out to plan where the needs exist and how they might be met. It is not the purpose of this book to list all of the legal steps and liabilities. If you do go into urban renewal, you will need to have a lawyer at your elbow most of the time.

The LPA—again speaking in generalities—acquires slum land by negotiation with its owners in most cases and by condemnation if that fails. Then it might be left with patches of raw land, a population which has been moved out to make room for the building of tomorrow's better city, and a big question at the moment: Where do we go now?

Here you, as a hopeful developer, can step in.

Keeping in mind that your attorney will probably be your best friend through all of the dealings you'll have with local, state, and federal authorities—certainly he is likely to be the human being in whose company, after your spouse, you will spend the most time during the initial stages—you'll come up with a plan. The plan should provide for meeting local building codes. It should provide something many times better in the way of accommodation than property which was removed. It will have to fit in with the community's master plan. It should dovetail with any planned civic services such as sewerage or new utility lines.

You will want to know what your tax situation will be when you're through. The general expectation is that many of these renewal plans should qualify for at least limited tax abatement.

If all goes well, and your harried lawyer has performed the proper legal steps, then you will probably be able to buy some of that land at a price lower than the LPA paid to get it. Such inducement is offered in order to make the needed improvements in living standards come about.

Not all urban renewal will be on this governmental scale, but it is all likely to call for bigger amounts of cash than you would require for downpayment on the Eagle Street residence or for swinging a block of moderately priced common stocks.

Private urban renewal projects have ranged from the ambitious Laclede Square urban rebirth in St. Louis, to individual

rehabilitations of old tenement buildings (which property owners with civic conscience plus an eye to leveraged profits have
undertaken all over the land), to the neighborhood rebuild-
ing of men like Sam Menszer.

TO RECAP:

1. All projections and the estimates of informed people say
that the decade of the seventies will be the biggest period of
housing construction ever seen. The need is there for removal
of low-grade housing. There is also demand building to put
walls around and roofs over other segments of our fast-expand-
ing population.

2. Repair and remodeling of existing housing will be a part
of the vast total of construction in the next ten years. This offers unusual leverage and opportunity for wealth seekers.

3. There is a new movement of people underway. The last
big tide took middle-class families out of the crowded central
cities and into suburban communities. That tide still flows
strongly. But countering it is a tinier trend, still a trickle but
giving signs of soon becoming larger, back to the old neighborhoods where there are convenient corner stores, accessible
public transportation, schools within walking distance, and all
of the other amenities of the bigger city.

4. Renewing entire older sections can offer wide profit opportunity. Sometimes, this takes the form of formal urban renewal. Many believe this may transform the faces of our cities
as the Employment Act, unnoticed when it was passed, transformed our economy.

5. Private developers have taken old, rundown neighborhoods in small towns or on the fringes of the cities and, at
moderate cost, spruced them up, adding to their saleability, to
their rental value, and, not least, to the pride of the people
who live in them.

6. A frequent kind of individualized urban renewal takes the form of finding houses which have been allowed to sink below the values of the structures which surround them. When a remodeler correctly judges the value of the area and the marketability of its property, fast doubling of invested money can come about.

7. Such a house must be carefully judged. A bargain, say people who do this kind of work, is one which is low enough in cost and has sufficient borrowability that an investor can put minimum money down to swing the deal, use only a part of capital to leverage his remodeling, then achieve a doubling of capital actually in use. Houses in need of extensive structural repair should be avoided as vehicles for quick fortune-building.

8. An investor cannot enter urban renewal with only a few thousand dollars. Yet, with $30,000 to $50,000 he can sometimes, says one who is professionally in the field, realize a fortune at a single stroke.

7

High Profits from High Rise

It was a dismal winter day. The rain was falling steadily outside and passersby turned up their collars against a wind that knifed through clothing as easily as an electric blade cuts slices from the side of tender roast. George stared out of his office window into the gray city scene. Then he swung around, put his feet on the desk, and dialed a number.

"That you, Ronald?" he asked. "Got an idea. Do you want to listen? I've been staring at that stodgy, shabby old building across the street. Someone told me it is up for sale. If it's at the right price, a relatively few bucks could fix it up, and then you and I might be on the road to a full-fledged big fortune. Want to go into the deal with me?"

This chapter takes us—you, George, and me—into the big leagues of real estate. It will be about apartments, office buildings, and shopping centers, all of which take more than a spare nickel or two to play with, but all of which can be leveraged, and each of which offers big-league profit opportunities for wealth-building commensurate with the sometimes big-league price tags needed to participate in the play.

The action certainly is big league. Consider Bob and Larry Tisch.

Loew's, Inc., is an $800 million firm that in its present state is the lengthened shadow of the Tisch brothers. They began with one New Jersey hotel. In its issue of April 12, 1969, *Business Week* described the Tisch successes with real estate deals on big property:

> In 20 years, Loew's chairman Laurence Alan Tisch, 45, and President Preston Robert Tisch, 42, have assembled a company grossing $800 million a year in 16 hotels, 110 movie theatres, real estate, and more recently, tobacco. They have achieved this essentially by acquiring and revitalizing undervalued properties. . . . To appreciate how far the Tisches truly have come, one has to hark back to [the] early postwar period. Their father, Al (who died in 1960) and their mother, Sadye, a formidable business person in her own right, sold the summer camp and family clothing concern and, in 1946, bought the Laurel-in-the-Pines at Lakewood, N.J. Interestingly, the property was discovered by Larry in a classified ad. By 1948, the hotel had been turned over to the boy prodigies, then out of college.
>
> The brothers beefed up the menu and jazzed up the entertainment at the Laurel-in-the-Pines, and soon were able to take over a couple of other small New Jersey hotels. By 1956 when they were 30 and 33 years old, they were able to build the $17 million Americana Hotel in Bal Harbour, Fla.—without a mortgage. . . . In 1956, the Tisches launched into a total new situation. . . . Acquisition of Loew's Theatres, Inc., then being spun off from the MGM company by court decree, provided the opportunity.

Everybody can't be a Tisch. But the opportunities which brought about the tremendous burst in Tisch personal and corporate fortunes are still there.

Certain things are common to all successful plays in large real estate such as theaters, motels, office buildings, apartment structures, and shopping centers. The latter three fall generally into the area of investment, although each calls for a degree of operational expertise, while theaters and mass-lodging institutions are operating businesses like department stores, copper mines, or automobile plants.

A common factor to most investment plays in this big market is that the investor doesn't buy to achieve rents. His aim is capital gains, and he uses some of the built-in accounting advantages of real estate to turn all or most of his ordinary income, taxable at top rates, into lower-taxed capital gains. It is possible that new federal legislation may inhibit this process in the future. But it is not likely to wipe it out. The name of the game, for investors if not for those who operate businesses based on real estate, is *resell*.

"Nice thing about what we are going to do with that office building," George noted as the two ordered lunch in a downtown restaurant, "is the writeoff it gives. Our income won't have to go through the Internal Revenue collector's mill. Eventually, of course, it shows up. But when it reappears, it does so as capital gains rather than high-taxed ordinary income.

"Let's say we go ahead with that building, and that we pay $800,00 to get it. We have to pay another $200,000 to make it modern and competitive with all the steel and glass showcases that are going up around it. Now we have invested $1 million. Probably, we'd be able to swing the deal, if money is not too tight, for about $70,000.

"Thus we have an $800,000 original cost which we might have to depreciate over a lengthy period. Say we can recover an average of about $55,000 every year as depreciation deduction on the original cost. The accountants will have to decide which method of depreciation would be most advantageous.

Another $40,000 could probably be lopped off in average yearly depreciation on the improvements since these would be able to go on a shorter timetable.

"Now look at potential rents. We have about 15,350 square feet of floor space. This counts store areas on the ground level which ought to bring higher rental once the building is polished and made to look like something out of a later era than that of Teddy Roosevelt. We can probably average $6.50 per square foot in rents. That would be a $99,775 annual income. Round it off to $100,000 to make the figuring easier.

"So here is $100,000 in income.

"The depreciation deduction of $95,000 every year will serve to wipe out all but 5 percent of the rental income, even before we have counted in overhead, debt service, and the like.

"However, that $95,000 deduction is not a gift. It has to be taken off the cost of the building. Say we hold the building for five years and then, if real estate prices have gone up as they usually do, and as prospects for inflation make it probable they will continue to do, we might receive $1,500,000 for the George and Ronnie Building."

Received for building	$1,500,000
Cost of building	
(original $1 million	
cost less depreciation	
of $95,000 per year)	525,000
Profit	$ 975,000

"Thus, instead of paying high income taxes on rental income of $95,000 each year, we would at one swoop make capital gains tax on $475,000—*but* at a sufficiently lower rate to result in substantial saving. The other $500,000 would be from 'real' profit on the building and also taxable at minimum capital gains rates.

"Remember that actual out-of-bank-account investment in this structure won't be the $1 million on which it will be depreciated. We will have put out approximately $70,000 to swing the deal after money is borrowed for leverage. So profit will be whopping—all nice, juicy, bankable capital gains!"

Whether the big-time property consists of apartments, store locations, or office space, the smart investor aims to rent most of it before he begins construction. If he remodels an older structure, he does the same thing. The play here is too big to justify much chance-taking.

Recently, the Federal Reserve Board commissioned, and the Urban Land Institute published, a study on *The Boom in Office Buildings.** Subtitled *An economic study of the past two decades,* it was prepared by Robert Moore Fisher, senior economist of the Federal Reserve Board.

He noted:

> Advance leasing of office space for future delivery is a common feature of the market. This practice is possible because tenant needs for accommodation can often be scheduled ahead with certainty. And they can be postponed temporarily by crowding up in current quarters.
>
> For office floor space in new buildings, advance leasing may proceed many months—if not a year or more—prior to opening. Once completed, new buildings with preleased floor space can begin operations with assurance of some current income. This is the very time, of course, when operating expenses are starting up and pressures would otherwise be mounting for quick lease negotiations on terms that might be less favorable for landlords.
>
> Advance leasing of new floor space allows future additions to the local supply of immediately-available floor space to be absorbed gradually. It eases the market shock that could occur if all newly-finished floor space were first thrown on the market only at the time of completion.
>
> Substantial leasing of floor space in new private buildings is often—but not invariably—a prerequisite to permanent financ-

---

* Reprinted by permission from ULI Technical Bulletin 58, *The Boom in Office Buildings.* Copyright 1967 by ULI—the Urban Land Institute, 1200 18th St. N.W., Washington, D.C. 20036.

ing. This requirement shifts some of the financial risk of successful operation from permanent lenders to construction lenders. It tends to encourage owners of new buildings to grant concessions and to assume the unexpired leases of incoming tenants, if necessary, in order to build up occupancy quickly. These and other practices make for negotiated leasing contracts and rental quotations that are far from standardized in all details.

Behind the boom in office and building construction, noted Mr. Fisher, lies the proliferation of paperwork that has characterized our times. "The postwar upsurge in demand for floor space in office buildings," said Mr. Fisher, "appears to reflect three main influences."

> First, there has been a sharp increase in the total volume of office activities. Despite growing use of electronic computers and other office equipment, this increase has been accompanied by a rapid expansion in employment of office workers. Second, there has probably been an increase in the share of total office activities and total office employment that has been accommodated in office buildings rather than in other kinds of facilities. Third, there appears to have been an increase in the average amount of floor space occupied per worker in office buildings, partly to provide room for more office machines and equipment.

While it appears that the growth of the immediate need for office space is slackening, the Urban Land Institute study noted that in the longer-term future, "stimulus to the . . . demand for office floor space will arise from further branching and mergers by private and public establishments as well as from more general requirements of growth. Such changes may often be accommodated best in new buildings with adequate floor space available to consolidate the operations of merged or expanded tenants."

It is well to know, however, that no overall national trend is going to make profits automatic. Before erecting a new building or remodeling that promising old structure which seems to need only cosmetic treatment to become metamorphized into a raving profit beauty, you and George might well ask certain questions:

What Is the Average Vacancy Rate in This Area?   You could check on this the easy way. Call the Chamber of Commerce and say: "How are you, Joe? Tell me something. What do office building vacancies run right now?" However, the answer to that easy way question is likely to be as valuable a piece of information as the knowledge that Joe Blow batted .198 for the Baltimore Orioles in 1899. You need instead to find out what vacancy rates are running for office buildings of *this* type, at *this* age, in *this* area. Suburban office vacancies might be higher or lower, depending upon the community, than downtown rates. Inside the business district, vacancies could be high on older buildings, no matter how cunningly remodeled, lower on new buildings. Or they could be the other way around. For your city, the neighborhood and street you consider, and the type of office, a knowledge of what occupancy rate you might expect should be considered in the light of a further question:

What Occupancy Rate Will Let Me Break Even?   It takes careful figuring of known and expected costs to obtain this figure, establish a rate based upon square footage of floor space, and know just what occupancy will provide break-even. "If a speculator expects to sell his building in a few years he has to first make it profitable so a new owner will be interested," observed one real estate pro with whom I discussed this.

Do We Furnish Janitorial or Maid Service?   Competition will determine this. If other office structures with which the proposed George and Ronnie Building competes furnish service to tenants, then George and Ronnie will do so or do without tenants. Addition of such a service can run up operating costs and must be taken into account in figuring break-even point.

Add Off-street Parking? It is doubtful that any single feature can give more attraction to a new or remodeled building than that of having a known parking space waiting for the harried tenant, bedeviled by freeway jams and distraught at the daily search for an open parking lot.

But space must be there, either in the form of land which can be paved over and marked off with yellow striping or in the form of lower floors which can be opened up to be used for cars. There is a nice economic point here. Will the added attraction of the building make possible rentals high enough to offset the loss of revenue from the parking floors? Will you be able to assess a parking fee?

Availability of off-street parking is a factor in other big-time land uses. With apartment houses, it is often a must. City planning codes, zoning regulations, and just plain common sense say that you may not build anything that attracts masses of cars without providing some places other than the clogged street where owners may park their vehicles.

In many ways, the economics of an apartment building are not greatly different from those of an office highrise. But there remains considerable difference, and you can't go into this field without becoming aware that, even within it, there is no uniformity. Apartments just aren't like each other. There are many types, no more alike than German shepherds, beagles, poodles, and cocker spaniels, all of which are canines.

Some Are Condominiums and Cooperatives According to the Cooperative League of the U.S.A., a housing co-op is defined this way: ". . . families work together to own and control their environment. Members buy shares in the cooperative corporation, which holds legal title to the entire development and signs for the mortgage that provides part of the financing.

Members also sign an occupancy agreement that establishes each family's right to occupy a specific dwelling and spells out occupancy rules."

In a cooperative, the tenant is part owner of a corporation. The corporation is the owner, operator, mortgagee, and generalissimo of the apartment dwelling.

A condominium is a different critter. Each tenant owns his own particular little part of the building, just as he would own a home and its surrounding land in a suburban subdivision. Someone once called a condominium a "subdivision in the sky." This is not a bad definition. The condominium owner undertakes to share certain common costs with his brother tenants. These typically include elevator service, building maintenance and upkeep, pruning and making pretty any outside garden area. In an article in the October, 1968, issue of *Buildings* magazine, Daniel S. Berman pointed out that "the condominium is new only to this country. Legal references go back to manuscripts of monks and to real estate devices of ancient Egypt and Rome."

Condominiums and cooperatives are sometimes of vast size. Co-op City in the Bronx is planned to have 15,382 apartments; its own shopping center; garage and recreational facilities; and a twenty-six-acre campus with a high school, two junior highs, and two elementary schools. It will cost nearly $300 million when finished. Fifty to fifty-five thousand people will live there, according to plans. Many a community calls itself a city and boasts of a population smaller than that.

Some Apartments Are for Only Certain Kinds of Tenants   Among the biggest opportunities are units—occasionally clusters of facilities nearly as vast as Co-op City—built for what our society has come to call "senior citizens." These might be run with or without medical and nursing care. There is a lot of money to be made in this market. But it is a specialized one, requiring different planning from that of a conventional apartment. You also need a different plan to operate at the other end of the age scale.

In this era when young people become independent earlier than their war-and-depression-fettered parents, there is a tendency for birds to leave their home nests earlier. They go away to college, become accustomed to dormitory life with rules different from those at home. Then they come back and find they don't like it. Many move out.

Seeing this movement, some smart real estate people have set up the "Swinging Apartment." This limits its tenants to young adults only. (A few allow unmarrieds only, and one magazine article called such as these "The Seduction Pad Arms.") Whatever you call them, they are a big thing and growing fast. Apartments for swinging singles are usually furnished, always have swimming pools, and occasionally supply piped-in music as well. Additional frills are at owners' discretion and tenants' demand.

And Then There Are the Recognizable Apartments Which Cater to Run-of-mill Families   Some are so expensive that the mill from which tenants run has to be a gold-lined one. Others operate at the lower end of the dollar scale, and between these cost extremes is the big part of the apartment market. Some cities and towns are too small to support senior citizen units—these usually go best in the sunny-climate states—and some lack enough young people ("young" in apartment lingo can mean anyone over sixteen and under fifty-six) to make specialized housing make dollar sense. But every community can support the good old "Standard Arms."

A common set of economic facts is likely to govern all kinds of apartment operation, however.

First, wear and tear, smudged walls, knocked-down doors, even plain maliciousness is probably going to be much higher in an apartment structure than an office building. Although the senior citizens as a group tend to do less damage than the junior swingers, people in the business say that an owner can expect heightened wear and tear from both. Rents and your cost estimates should take this into account. A rule of thumb is that if you keep overhead expense ratio at one-third of income, you will do well.

Second, you probably need a return of 10 percent annually on investment to come out profitably. Like most rules of thumb, this is not guaranteed to produce a profit. But the apartment which costs $1 million and produces $100,000 annually in rent is likely to be one whose owner is able to afford Florida winters and the other perquisites of affluence.

Moreover, the same rule of thumb says that on the average you should have about 10 percent vacancies. If you run a 10 percent vacancy rate and still are able to bring in 10 percent of cost in rental income, you should stay among those wintering in Florida and enjoying occasional summers in Europe as befits a traveler well along on the real estate Road to Wealth.

But nothing runs itself. And the fourth rule for success is that someone has to be on hand to mind the store. Obviously, if you are wintering in a sun clime and summering in a cold one, it will be hard to commute every evening. So you may need a good live-in manager. Such a manager nearly always gets free rent. He may or may not additionally receive a salary, and the salary, if he gets one, may be large, small, or somewhere in between. That is dependent on the size of the job to be done and how well you can negotiate with your prospective managerial talent.

A fifth rule is that cash flow matters more than net profits. Cash flow is the amount of "gross" profit before such sophisticated items as depreciation are deducted. This point is obvious if you keep in mind that the smart investor in highrise real estate is looking to convert rents into capital gains, not to realize high-taxed ordinary income. Aim, therefore, for a sizable cash flow. The net income figure at the bottom is less important.

To get this cash flow, you have to watch rule six, which states that a neighborhood will only support one level of rents. If a square-footage figure you have in mind to produce the needed 10 percent of cost each year isn't one that applies to other places in the immediate neighborhood, most people with experience will shake their heads and say, "Poor George. He is not going to make it asking high rents in a medium-rent district."

A seventh rule states that if you can't build in newness, you should build in charm. Older structures can't always be given the look of those out of which carpenters, plumbers, and glaziers walked only yesterday. But charm—that's another thing. Women of fifty frequently have more of it than willowy lasses of twenty. Apartments can be given the charm treatment, too. And like the winning woman of fifty, they sometimes attract more admirers than the jet set lady in the miniskirt.

Put in a pool, says the eighth rule. People who live in apartments like to be around other people, while those who feel fenced in with fellow humans close by opt for the wide open suburbs. And so the pool becomes the center of the modern apartment house. A pool usable all year is an almost sure attraction.

"Best $8,000 we ever spent," says one apartment owner who at first argued when he found that his architect's plans included a swimming area.

Take cognizance of the view, is the message of rule nine. If your structure is amid handsome surroundings, every advantage should be taken of it. But if it looks over brick kilns, semi-slums, or the city dump a half mile away, then shrubbery might hide the near-in nuisances, while windowless walls keep people on the upper floors from looking out over a poor view.

Food vending areas and coin-op equipment such as clothes washers and driers can be an added revenue source. But if they cheapen the place, or fail to fit in with its decor and plan, then the extra income might be bought at a high price.

There is no "right" or "wrong" answer here. It will depend upon the setup and tenants' wants and demands.

The tenth and final consideration is a ticklish one. On it may depend whether you will winter each year in a sunny climate, or go flat, cold broke. That consideration is the political climate.

How badly this can affect apartment owners' profit hopes can be seen from recent experience in New York City. In its July, 1969, *Monthly Economic Letter,* the First National City Bank noted what it called "the twilight of New York's private housing market." The study pointed out:

> The New York City rent control law permits landlords to increase rents by 15 percent when apartments are vacated and re-rented. Those tenants, however, who have stayed in an apartment for a long period find their rents falling further and further below the free market level and consequently have little incentive to move. This tends to limit labor and family mobility. With rent control benefits based largely on duration of occupancy, the law inadvertently discriminates against the poor blacks and the Puerto Ricans who tend to be new on the urban scene. Moreover, since smaller families are understandably reluctant to leave large, controlled apartments, these newer families, which tend to be fairly large, are denied access to the more spacious apartments they might find more easily in a free housing market.
>
> Yield limitations under rent controls induce landlords to cut corners in building maintenance, thus contributing to relatively rapid housing deterioration. Furthermore, because attractive returns are possible on investments in commercial development and in housing elsewhere in the nation, responsible property owners and financial institutions tend to withdraw their connection with properties subject to public price administration. Then less skilled or unscrupulous operators take over. . . . The inevitable results are excessive code violations, suspension of rent payments, and abandonment, to the detriment of all concerned.
>
> . . . the battery of obstacles facing New York's free housing market has all but eliminated the conventional entrepreneur-

developer of multiple housing who selects the site, acquires capital, arranges construction contracts, operates and manages the property.

Happily, such problems as face New York dwelling owners are absent from other parts of the country. And nowhere are they part of the booming shopping center field. The most obvious fact about shopping centers today is that they are b-i-g. Some are extra big. A number are very big. A few are super-big. The little old neighborhood center with a collection of Mom and Pop stores clustered around a smallish Woolworth's is as dead today as the Mom and Pop "tourist cabin" court which has been effectively replaced by shining new motels that have everything an in-city hotel offers.

Recently, the Urban Land Institute issued a study called *The Dollars and Cents of Shopping Centers: 1969.** This study pointed out that

> A regional shopping center provides a variety and depth of "shopping goods" comparable to a central business district, including general merchandise, apparel, and home furnishings, as well as a variety of services, and may include recreational facilities. One or more department stores are the principal tenants of a regional center. Each full-line department store has generally a gross leasable area of not less than 100,000 square feet.

The ULI study divided centers into three groups. Regional centers such as the type described above attract thousands. Median size for these is over 500,000 square feet. Some regional centers have malls with all-weather air conditioning. A community center is smaller than this. It might run around 150,-000 square feet (median) and offer wide convenience goods along with some larger stores such as a furniture-appliance outlet or a junior department store. These often have profes-

---

*Reprinted by permission from *The Dollars and Cents of Shopping Centers: 1969*. Copyright 1969 by ULI—the Urban Land Institute, 1200 18th St. N.W., Washington, D.C. 20036.

sional offices as well. The baby of the group—but a potent moneymaker despite its size—is what the ULI calls a neighborhood center, embracing about 58,000 square feet (median) with convenience goods and services only. Usually a supermarket food store is the hub around which this center revolves.

The trend among the bigger centers is toward the enclosed, all-weather mall. Of 101 regional centers in the Urban Land Institute's survey, 36 offered air-conditioned malls, and results were usually higher for these. The August, 1968, issue of *Buildings* magazine reported on conversion of a big Kansas City center, The Landing, to mall air conditioning. "Sales volume," said the article, "shows a definite upward trend. And when Kansas City temperatures move into the mid-90's or higher, customers report that The Landing is a pleasant shopping experience."

A complete breakdown of what income you might expect from each of the three types is available in *The Dollars and Cents of Shopping Centers: 1969*.

Maybe by this time you are sold on centers. It will be a George and Ronnie Center instead of the George and Ronnie Arms or the George and Ronnie Building in the heart of downtown. How do you start such a mammoth project?

Experts recommend that you do so the same way you would begin any other project. Study the field, the need, the prospects for profit. *Buildings* magazine, in its issue of August, 1968, devoted to shopping centers, proposed that advance study steps include the following:

   1. A trade area, based on familiarity with the trade areas of many similar shopping centers *and based upon application of the similarities to the specific situation at hand.* [Italics supplied.]
   2. Calculating present and projected future population.
   3. Projecting per capital expenditures (in real terms excluding inflation).
   4. Calculating a sales potential.

5. Taking a suburban share; that is, estimating the future split of total sales potential between downtown and suburban stores.

6. Estimating a site share; that is, predicting the percentage of suburban sales potential the subject center might be able to get against its competition.

Aware that the object of shopping center operation is not achievement of architectural excellence or even of shopper attraction alone, the *Buildings* study went on to note that

. . . a proposed shopping center can have a glorious market but a disastrous financial picture. Even a deal with potentially good financial results can get out of hand unless there is a firm policy from the beginning on rent and allowances, costs and expenses for the guidance of architects, engineers and leasing people and the others on the development team.

The study proposed that additional study steps include:

7. Estimated rents, both percentage and guaranteed, together with estimated volume of business that might be produced by each store under normal operating conditions.

8. The financial results of project development with estimates of income, expenses and costs.

9. Consideration of all of the detail that needs to be resolved in almost every project (e.g., what is the most we should pay for additional land, should the mall be open or closed, etc.).

Whether your project—office building, shopping center, or apartment highrise—eventually proves the best deal you ever entered or the worst turkey ever hung around anybody's neck, will depend partly upon the leases you sign. The target may be eventual sale for capital gain, and the heck with the rents. But a later sale will depend on how profitable that G&R Building is as a going proposition. Consult an attorney before drawing up any lease form. But remember to have these points included as a minimum for protection of both landlord and tenant:

- Names of the parties to the contract.
- Description of the place you're renting.
- Length of lease, when it begins, when it ends.
- The amount of rent and how it is to be paid. (Sometimes first and last months are paid together.)
- Where rent is to be paid (usually your office, sometimes the office of rental agent or manager).
- The use to which the lessee will put your property (kind of store or office, business activity permissible in the case of an apartment, residential).
- Condition it is in when turned over to tenant.
- Who is responsible for maintenance (spell out item by item).
- Who pays utility bills.
- Condition in which lessee agrees to leave property on lease expiration.
- Provisions for what occurs should delays in occupancy crop up.
- Any improvements and changes you agree to make for the tenant.
- Whether tenant is allowed to make changes on his own and what changes are permissible.
- Who is responsible for damages. (Spell out the kinds of damages.)
- Whether signs or other advertising will be permitted. Restrictions on size of these if any.
- Provision for showing property to prospective tenants if tenant vacates.
- Provision for notification of intention to move or stay on expiration of lease.
- Option (provisional) for tenant to renew.
- Rules for surrender at the end of the lease period.
- Subleasing conditions if any.
- Insurance payment responsibilities—yours or his?
- What happens if rent becomes delinquent.

■ Fires or "acts of God."

■ Provision for collection fees if required.

TO RECAP:

1. Apartment buildings, office buildings, and shopping centers are the big wide "Interstates" of the real estate Roads to Wealth. They are expensive of access. But they will carry you far and fast.

2. In this field, many successful fortune builders do not invest to achieve rental income. Their aim is to turn rents—taxed as ordinary income—into capital gains, taxed at a lower rate.

3. In this big-league real estate play, as in other ways to wealth, leverage plays a key role.

4. Advance renting of space is a step to success, not only assuring occupancy but also facilitating the financing on which leverage is based.

5. Surveys have shown a probably high continuing need for all three types of buildings in the years ahead.

6. But no overall national trend can guarantee that a given project will be profitable. If you are considering the big building field, you should survey vacancy rates in the area where you plan to build, determine what vacancy rate will let your project break even; whether you should run up overhead but possibly increase tenant attractiveness by providing extra services; the requirements and cost for off-street parking; the kinds of tenants you wish to attract; the kind of upkeep you can expect to do.

7. Most big buildings require a staff and, unless you are going to put in a great deal of your own time, a manager.

8. Cash flow is more important than net profit.

9. Shopping centers have grown into vast, multicompany shopping areas of as much as 500,000 square feet. There are

opportunities also in smaller community and neighborhood shopping centers.

10. The prevailing political climate and the attitudes of regulatory authorities determine whether a community is one in which certain kinds of structures will be profitable.

8

Wheat to Wool —
the Commodity Road

SOYBEANS, HOG BELLIES, silver, palladium, plywood, wheat, corn, frozen eggs, cocoa, grease wool, orange juice, broilers, hides—these are certainly not glamorous things as are office buildings, tracts of raw land, or go-go mutual funds and stocks. But they can be highly profitable possessions none the less.

Once upon a time, the processors of food products faced severe pricing problems. A candy maker might receive an order for X number of cars of peanut brittle deliverable in six months. He could not deliver it earlier than that. So he could not make it in advance.

The price he had quoted was based upon today's price for sugar and peanuts. Yet buying "spot" raw materials wasn't practical. Since the candy would not be manufactured for months, there would be sizable charges for warehouse rent and possible warehouse losses from pilferage, fire, and flood, before the time came to utilize the raw commodities. If he waited until the commodities were needed before he bought them, he might find them lower in price. In that event, his profits on the peanut brittle would be enhanced. But the raw materials might have gone up by then, and his profit might vanish or even turn into a loss.

It was quite a problem. The facts of life before futures contracts were invented forced users of commodities—ranging from soybeans to silver, copper to cold-storage eggs, hides to hogs, wool to wheat—willy-nilly into the field of commodity speculation. Many a hapless manufacturer found himself wildly successful in his main business but dead broke because of a mistake in judgment regarding future raw material prices. Some mechanism was needed to "hedge" against either loss or gain.

At the time our candy manufacturer was mulling over this problem there lived nearby a farmer brighter than his brethren who saw the plight of the food processor, but had scant time for sympathy with his colleague since he, too, faced a problem. The market for his sugar and other produce was a good one at the moment. But it might drop, he feared, by the time he brought the harvest to market. Farmer Frank wanted to nail down today's price so that he could budget his affairs for the year and establish whether or not the family could afford to buy the newest model buggy horse fully loaded with automatic blinders, power harness, and one of the newfangled music boxes such as his neighbor down in the next county had bought.

Farmer Frank and Candymaker Carl met in town one day and began sharing their troubles over a beer at Sam's Saloon where the best free lunch in town was offered with every nickel glass of suds. (They don't make bargains like that any more.)

"Tell you what, Carl," said Frank. "You need a lot of sugar. I will have a lot of sugar to sell in the fall. I'll sell it to you now. Then you will know how much your sugar costs come fall. If sugar is higher than today's level, you will make something on inventory. If it is lower, you can buy at the market, pegging down a lower price, and then sell my futures contract at a loss. The amount you make by having lower-priced sugar come fall will be balanced by the amount you lose when you sell my futures contract at a correspondingly lower price. It won't make you richer, but it will save you from becoming poorer. And I will know exactly how much our sugar income will be this year so I can put in the order at Luke's Livery Stable for that fully loaded buggy puller with automatic blinders, power harness, and a music box.

"Is it a deal?"

And so from arrangements probably not greatly different from that was born commodity futures trading. It began as a hedging plan to free producers and users of commodities from the vagaries of the pricing mechanism so that when they had to stand or fall upon the ability to deliver a profitable product in the future, the platform on which they stood would have at least one wobble—that of changing and sometimes unpredictable prices—removed.

The above is a deliberately oversimplified explanation of a complicated kind of marketing operation. As soon as the simple kind of producer-user "futures" contract was born, a further problem arose. Both men wanted to eliminate risk which was a built-in, integral part of the setup. But if nobody was willing to take a chance, would the risk vanish? It was found that the risk unobligingly refused to efface itself. The hot potato of risk had to be in someone's hands.

Enter the speculator.

Sometimes he is called a "speculator." Sometimes he likes to term himself a "commodity investor." Many people speak of him as a "trader." Whatever you call him, he is the one in whose hand the hot potato rests.

Remember that fact if you go into commodity speculation as a Road to Wealth. A Road to Wealth it has indeed been for many people, a road permitting rapid travel and provided with gigantic leverage poles to help the travelers who use it to leap over all kinds of capital obstacles. But it carries big risks, too.

If you run a restaurant and buy eggs, you get them from a wholesale house. The actual eggs, physically present in containers, are trucked from the distributor's warehouse to your restaurant door.

But if you are interested in eggs as a speculation instead of a raw material for your customers' morning omelets, the probabilities are you will never see an egg, open a carton, or crack a shell. You own something called a "contract." The contract will be for a set amount of eggs—a startlingly large amount, in fact—deliverable in a certain month, December, for example.

This contract means that in December you are to obtain delivery on *18,000 dozen* fresh eggs, enough to make omelets by the carload. Suppose, as many a commodity speculator has dreamed on nightmarish occasions, I should have to take delivery on all those eggs? Would someone back up a truck to my front door and let them slide down on the grass and across my front steps? What would I do with 18,000 dozen eggs?

In practice, speculators seldom, if ever, let a contract go that far. It can always be sold (and should always be sold if you're speculating in eggs and not making omelets out of them) in the early days of the month when they become "spot." Even if you were to take delivery on all of those eggs, you would not receive a lawnful of hen products, but rather a warehouse receipt evidencing ownership of the commodity. You would then begin paying storage charges. And you would have to make a substantial further payment since all you put in initially was margin. *If* you let things go so far.

You would have bought that contract in the expectation of a rise in price. The leverage in such a contract is fantastic. The whole bag of eggs—the contract—entails a lot of money. But the margin needed to swing a contract is small. The exact amount varies. Many brokerage houses like to have an extra margin of safety, so they permit only margin which is fractionally higher than other brokers' minimum margins. For purposes of figuring here, we will consider that most margin is 10 percent. When you engage in actual trading, ask your brokerage firm what margin it expects. If the margin is above minimum, and you don't like things that way, you can always shop around for another broker whose notions are more liberal.

Commissions are set by the exchanges on which commodities trade. These are principally in New York and Chicago. Smaller exchanges also exist, but most trading is done on the big ones. Eggs, for example, are generally traded on the Chicago Mercantile Exchange. Commission on eggs is $33 per contract plus $3 clearance fee—$36. The commission is assessed only for the complete transaction, buy and sell orders together.

We noted that your theoretical egg contract was purchased in the hope that eggs would go up. Let's say you were right. They went up by 3 cents a dozen. Then you would have made a gross profit of $540, less the $36 commission for a net of $504 on each contract you bought. That does not seem so large in relation to the total value of 18,000 dozen eggs, whether made into omelets or not.

But look at it as a percentage of $800 put up as margin to swing the contract. That is a profit of 63 percent. Commodities usually move fast. However, let's say this was a slow swing in prices. It took three months to build that profit. If you annualize 63 percent made in three months, it comes to yearly rate of profit of 252 percent.

Pretty profits like that make commodity trading a real Road to Wealth.

And you can make it both ways. It is as easy for you or George to sell eggs short as it is to buy them. You are not dealing in the actual eggs and, unless you let things go too far into the delivery month, you do not have to worry about having 18,000 dozen eggs to deliver to whoever was the other party to your transaction. So that, after your eggs reach what you consider a peak, if you are convinced that a down move equal to the up move is next on the bill of fare, you can sell short another contract and repeat the happy process (provided, of course, your judgment as to the next likely direction of egg prices proves to be a correct one).

These opportunities do not exist in eggs alone. The range of commodity trading is very wide. You can trade wheat, corn, oats, rye, soybeans, soybean meal, soybean oil, grain sorghums, barley, flaxseed, cattle, broilers, eggs, frozen pork bellies, hogs, potatoes (Idaho or Maine), sugar, cocoa, cotton, frozen concentrated orange juice, plywood, copper, silver, platinum, palladium, hides, and wool on active, liquid markets in New York, Chicago, Kansas City, Minneapolis, and Winnipeg.

There are some solid advantages to commodity trading. One is the liquidity of commodity markets. You don't have to advertise, buttonhole people, show houses, dream up concepts and ideas for adding value to land. You don't have to do anything to find customers when you are ready to sell or someone who wants to sell when you itch to buy. You can get in in the morning and if at noon you decide a mistake was made, you can be out by 12:01. You have a steady flow of information on which to base your decisions. You have leverage working for you to multiply profits so that even a little move can mean a big gain.

Not least, you have the volatility of commodities. Nobody waits very long to get rich (or, if he is wrong, to end up poorer after a transaction than he was when he entered it). Commodities *move*. Quickly.

Over the course of a six-month period, a swinging stock might double in price or, in a down market, it might conceivably lose half of its value in that time. Generally, it takes a swinger of a stock to show performance like this. But even a slow-moving pedestrian commodity might do as much in six weeks, remembering that we are discussing not a doubling in the price of the commodity, but in the capital which a trader would be employing for margin. A commodity which was swinging wildly and widely could do it in two weeks—even in one week—and occasionally and rarely, in a couple of days.

That's action.

But all of the features of the commodity road are not advantages. The marvelous leverage which makes profits grow so quickly can make losses loom as suddenly. However, if you're a smart trader, your loss need not be as large as the loss the commodity suffers.

A disadvantage, if you're seeking to follow this road while your main interest is centered on a full-time occupation elsewhere, is the amount of continuing study commodity success calls for. Study is necessary in real estate, stocks, bonds, and mutual funds. Because of the suddenness with which things happen in commodity trading, study must be daily, sometimes hourly. The curves in the road are frighteningly slick and deadly.

However, like highways on which cars and trucks travel, Roads to Wealth are seldom unsafe if the rules of safe driving are followed. For this particular road, the rules are:

■ *Drive only on the sunny days.* Go into a commodity situation only if the prospects for profit look overwhelmingly good. We will shortly consider the fundamental and technical criteria for determining this. There are always some situations that look good on one count, less shiny from another point of view, and it is natural for an enthusiastic trader (traders are enthusiastic people) to want to minimize the poor side while looking on the best face. That is a way to achieve mediocrity if you are fortunate and poverty if you are not. The commodity road offers enough pitfalls without adding to them by driving under conditions of half visibility.

Your commodity capital does not have to be at work all of the time. Wheel it out on the road only when the road conditions are sunniest.

■ *Never meet a margin call.* With margin small in relation to the overall value of the contract, a slight move in the direction you expect prices to go is enough to make a very big move in your profits. But a slight move the other way will eat sufficiently into capital for you to receive one of those nice, friendly phone calls one morning. "Hello, George?" the voice is likely to say. "This is Joe the margin clerk at Whoozis, Groovy, and Outerspace, your brokers. You need more margin on that contract of eggs. Please send X hundred dollars and let us have it this morning."

Don't write the check.

Just hang up.

If you hang up, Whoozis, Groovy, and Outerspace will sell out your position, and your margin, if not eaten entirely away, will be returned to you in depleted form.

Better depleted than no form. Better not to have another chunk eaten out of additional margin.

Better, in other words, a little loss than a big one. Experienced commodity traders make a fetish of never meeting a margin call. They reason that if things have gone so badly as to bring one of those gravelly voices onto the phone to ruin a morning, then they have gone badly enough to abandon the position, retreat, and come back with impaired but still effective capital to trade another day.

■ *Drive with both eyes open.* In looking at stocks, bonds,

and mutual funds in the earlier chapters, we determined that there are two types of study. The first is called "fundamental." It applies to a company and to the economy and to the probable supply and demand in markets for a company's products or services. The second discipline is called "technical." It applies to the supply-demand situation for stock certificates or for bonds, and its aim is to determine when the securities should be bought and sold.

It's that way in commodity study, too.

Some people are enthusiastic followers of one school of study. They tend to take their own thing seriously while deriding the kind of analysis followed by other analysts and traders who, in turn, laugh at the ways the first group do things. These investor-traders drive the road with one eye closed.

Results of that kind of driving are likely to be fully as hazardous as a one-eyed jaunt down a rapid interstate highway would be in an automobile.

■ *Don't push the accelerator all the way down.* Plungers are interesting people to watch. When they win, they pile up the money so fast that almost no one can count it, and fawning observers pat them on the back, invite them out for lunch to sell them new Cadillacs, and sometimes buy them drinks in the evening in the hope of getting tips.

But a plunger has to lose eventually if he keeps to his plunging ways. He can only be wrong once, and then he is wiped out.

Smart speculators always keep something back. A cash reserve is a handy thing to have against the time when the gravelly voice of Joe the margin clerk comes over your phone in the morning to tell you that Whoozis, Groovy, and Outerspace have had to sell you out and that only $5.68 remains of your $800 margin.

■ *Pour it on in the good stretches; go slow where the road is bumpy.* You win in commodities by following up success. Where the road is wide and smooth and traffic is not in your way, it is safe practice to push the speed needle up a few notches. If your commodity contracts are going your way, add to them. You will have the as yet unrealized profit from your first position to protect your second, and by following up success you will be moving in the smoothest path toward profits.

But go easy when the road becomes bumpy. There is temptation when things go badly to think: "Well, if I just buy another couple of contracts here, I will have reduced my average cost, and then it will only require a little nudge upward to put me even or even to make me a profit." That is equivalent to pushing harder on the accelerator when cars crowd up around you on the Interstate. People who average down are, in fact, increasing the commitment to a losing proposition. Instead of an initial profit to render the second purchase almost risk-free, as happens to the trader who follows success, these unwise and unwary people are averaging the cost downward, to be sure, but immediately have an average loss on the whole position.

That way lies not wealth, but inadequacy.

■ *Don't try to drive too many vehicles.* It is well to always keep many commodity situations under surveillance, but invest only in the best, the most promising one or two of the lot. Having fewer commitments is bound to sharpen your judgment. If nothing else, it will increase your eagerness to get out when an investment proves unprofitable. And in cutting losses, while letting profits run until they become sizable, you will have mastered the most vital and difficult rule of speculating successfully.

You should choose which commodities to trade by answering a number of questions. These include:

Q. *What is the background business climate?*

If recession looms, probabilities are that few things will go up. If a new boom appears to be beginning, it can carry commodity prices along in its wake particularly if, as usually happens, boom brings inflation. Economic criteria covered in earlier chapters should stand you in good stead and put you a few knowledge notches up on less learned commodity people.

But don't look only at the Stateside business climate. Many commodities move in international channels. A sizable part of the market for others is found overseas. Worldwide conditions should be weighed and judged.

Q. *What is probable production this year?*

How much crop carry-over from last year? Until a crop is in, or the amount of overseas commodity which will be marketed is known, this remains conjecture. After it is known, of course, it ceases to be a market factor affecting prices because the price structure will have already taken it into account. While you cannot know the future until it happens, you can use some knowledgeable appraisals of prospects which are issued by the U.S. Department of Agriculture. Many brokerage houses issue private appraisals from time to time.

(Your broker in commodities might be the same fellow who handles orders for stocks, bonds, convertibles, warrants, and mutual funds. Most bigger firms wear a number of hats and have research departments which peer as studiously into the wheat situation or the prospects for hog bellies as their analytical brethren across the hall do with corporate investment media. On the other hand, some speculators prefer to deal with brokerage firms that specialize in commodities. You pay your money in either case, and the choice is not good or bad in itself, but only insofar as it works well for you.)

Q. *What are demand prospects?*

Some you can appraise closely. This is true of commodities which have industrial uses. But sometimes appraisals are nothing but educated guesses. However, any serious appraisal is better than none, and if you do not feel able to decide how many million bushels of wheat will be shipped overseas and how many will end in the form of instant breakfast foods on your table in the morning, you might get the professional appraisals of three or four sources—taking in a commodity advisor or commodity market letter plus the research appraisals from brokerage sources—and average them off. Some traders say this is a sound way to do a job for which there is no scientific basis.

Q. *Can competitive products eat into the probable market?*

Soybean and other vegetable oils can be used almost alternatively. A scarcity situation in one will not automatically bring about higher prices as long as glut exists in the alternatives.

Q. *What is the current news saying?*

When Chile or Zambia decides to nationalize copper, the result might well be a future shortage. But not automatically. For if the nation which now controls the product should decide to meet an immediate capital need by flooding world markets from its stockpiles, the quicker result could be lower prices.

Governments' agricultural policies affect pricing and must be watched. Wars have widespread effects. Sometimes the chain reactions from shortages due to combat or destruction can widen out to touch unexpected commodities.

Currency devaluations act upon the ability of a country to buy American and Canadian commodities. They change the prices of products a nation exports. Usually the aim of devaluation is to make local products more competitive in global markets.

Q. *What are seasonal tendencies?*

Many commodities tend toward price weaknesses at certain seasons of the year, and their prices reach high levels at others. This tendency is seldom strong enough to make it the basis for a trading system in itself. But it exists and should be taken into account. No one wants to be long a commodity in May when the historic trend of May-to-July prices is downward.

If you study the six points above, you will have a good beginning on successful commodity speculation of the kind that can make a really small stake become a fortune in the pits where wheat, wool, and wealth sometimes mean the same thing.

But you will only have made a beginning. Armed with this information, you will have one eye open as you send the car screeching down the commodity road. To open the other eye, you will require a grasp of timing study.

This involves charts. To determine how effective charts really were in pinpointing profitable get-in and get-out spots with futures, I recently conducted a study on heavily traded commodities during a year which offered a microcosm of everything anyone could find in a trading twelve months. The year was 1967. There were wars and threats of more war, peace scares, diplomatic crises by the carton, monetary crises, surfeit, and shortage. Writing about this study of technical tools for the magazine *Successful Farming,* I reported:

> All of the recognized tools of timing study were stacked up against commodity market conditions and although not all of them proved to be worthwhile, there were sufficiently solid results to indicate that chart study methods can be adapted to commodity price forecasting. Thirty-five recognizable trades showed up in study of thirteen contracts during that peril-and-profit year of '67. Of these, twenty proved profitable, fifteen resulted in losses. I recently cited this finding to a friend. "What, only four out of seven were profit trades?" he asked. "That couldn't be worth doing." He felt differently when the dollar figures were cited.
>
> These showed that by trading one contract at a time, the 20 profit transactions would have yielded $13,916.00. The fifteen loss trades nicked $2,089.00 off that to give a net profit figure, exclusive of commissions, of $11,827.00. Taking profitable and unprofitable trades together, on average each of the thirty-five brought a gain of $337.91.

Thus a trader who had followed these methods would have been very, very right when he was right. Even in the minority of cases when he was wrong, his results would have been anything but horrid.

Overall results are summed up in the accompanying table.

SUMMARY OF COMMODITY TIMING SIGNALS

Type of signal	Profits	Losses	Percent-age of trade profits
Momentum—long term	$ 8,614.90 (10 trades)	$ 1,344.40 (3 trades)	· 77
New highs—new lows	11,274.50 (20 trades)	1,651.00 (15 trades)	57
Head and Shoulders	75.00 (1 trade)	none	100
Flags and pennants	519.00 (2 trades)	none	100
Stalemate breaks	2,074.50 (4 trades)	255.00 (3 trades)	57
Fanlines	none	183.00 (2 trades)	0

In *support-resistance level analysis* (which we looked at briefly in Chapter Three with regard to bonds) chartists use a vertical line on ruled paper to show price action of a futures contract for one day (Fig. 1). If the contract traded between a high of 2.40 and a low of 2.30, and the last trade of the day (the "close") was 2.35, the chartist would pencil a line from the horizontal area representing 2.30 to the area indicating 2.40 and put a small cross mark at 2.35 to show that was the last price of the day. Sometimes these lines which delineate price action touch the same upper level several times without penetrating through. Chartists then call the overhead level a "resistance line." A line against which declining prices battered without going through would be called a "support level." When prices suddenly zoom above a resistance level (or slice down below a support area), the chartist is led to buy (on the upward break) or sell (on a downward one) because he reasons that the resistance in the form of sell orders has been eaten through—or that support in the form of buy orders has

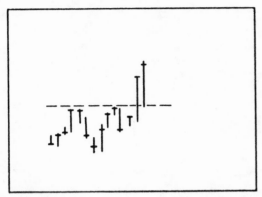

Figure 1 *Support-resistance breakout comes when prices have bumped many times against an overhead area (resistance) or a downslide level (support), then with a whoosh spurt out of the level which had previously stopped price movement. The presumption is that buying has eaten through the resistance of sellers in the case of an overhead breakout, or that selling proved stronger than the ability of bulls to buy in a support penetration.*

deteriorated—and therefore the balance between supply and demand has become an imbalance. Out of this imbalance, predictions as to possible future price movement can be made.

To guard against being wigwagged in or out by movements which in commodity markets would be minor and random, it was decided that for purposes of this study a "high" had to be the top of an upward swing lasting at least five trading days. A "low" had to be the bottom of a decline of the same length. One- or two-day movements are random even in fast-moving markets.

"Head and Shoulders" is another valuable timing tool for judging commodity price turns (Fig. 2). A typical H&S might occur at the high of a trend and warn of a probable turn coming. Upward trends do not go straight. They consist of rising zigs, called "rallies," followed by downward zags, called "reac-

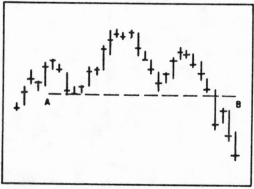

Figure 2 *"Head and Shoulders" pattern is found less often than amáteurs believe on a commodity chart. But it is an important timing tool. When a bottom H&S (the mirror image of this top Head and Shoulders) shows a signal by breaking of the "neckline"—line A–B—, then a buy signal has been given. On breaking of a top Head and Shoulders neckline comes the signal which says to liquidate long positions and to sell the commodity short.*

tions." While each upward zig carries higher than the zig before it, and each downward reactionary zag bottoms out higher than the bottom of the last zag before it—all is well. The chart paper will look as if an upward staircase had been drawn on it.

Now consider that a rally starts, goes some distance, peters out, and a reaction follows. So far all is normal. Another rally comes along and carries prices higher than the rally before. But it is succeeded by a reaction deeper than the zags that came earlier. This one goes down to about the same level as the preceding reaction. Now still another rally ensues, but it is tired and does not reach as high as the last one. Smart chart students watch things closely at such a point. Will the decline stop at the support level where two earlier declines bottomed? Or slice through?

If it slices through, a sell signal has been given.

The first rally was the left shoulder, the next the head, the third—the tired, weak little one—the right shoulder. When the "neckline" represented by the two valleys was violated, a bell had been rung.

Head and Shoulders formations are not found only at tops. They occur at bottoms as well. Reverse the description above and you have a bottom H&S signaling probable turn to a strong advance in the commodity's price.

The rounding turn is found infrequently, but where found is worth heeding. Prices during such a reversal form what some analysts call a "saucer" of gradually rounding action, pointing at last in a new direction. A rounding turn usually depicts tired market action. It is found at both tops, where it indicates a new trend downward, and bottoms, where it frequently signals a spirited advance coming.

Stalemates are very tiring things to live through. But out of this kind of movement come strong indications of subsequent price movements. Sometimes such a range takes the form of a triangle. At other times it is roughly rectangular in shape (Fig.3). On a few occasions it works out to look like a reversed triangle with the narrow end to the left of the chart watcher. Special names have been developed for each of these formations. But since they are all essentially the same, and are "read" by the same events, it is well to lump them together. Generally, an upward spurt out of the boundaries of a trading range indicates that an advance in prices, of probably worthwhile proportions, is likely to come about. A downward break from the boundaries of the broken stalemate area portends sadder days of lower prices.

Flags and pennants are sharp, short trading ranges which often come in the middle of a long-term trend, and thus give an advance hint of its probable extent. Timing students have a saying: "The flag flies at half mast." Flags and pennants work well in commodity timing, and one of their beauties is

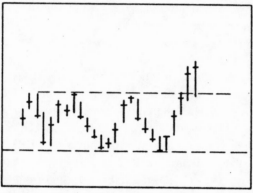

Figure 3   *Typical stalemated trading range might take a rectangular form such as this. Or it might be an ascending, descending, or symmetrical triangle. Occasionally it looks like an inverted triangle with the narrow part to the left. In any case, it represents an evenly balanced battle between buyers and sellers, neither of whom can push prices out of the stalemate. A breakout from one of these trading ranges often indicates a sizable movement in the direction of the breakout.*

that they allow a trader who missed the first signal to jump on for half a ride which, as with loaves, is better than no ride at all.

Fanlines (Fig. 4) are made by a series of three ever-flatter "trendlines" drawn to connect the top of an old up trend or the bottom of the last important down movements with new rally tops (in the case of a rise, reaction bottoms). The theory works often enough to be worth noting that when three such lines form a "fan" and are broken, indications of a trend change should be acted upon.

In Chapter Four, we ran into *momentum* study, which related what was happening to the asset values of mutual funds to what was occurring in the overall stock market. Momentum study is valuable with commodities, too.

The constant to which the price of a futures contract is related should be a yardstick intended to represent commodities in general. You can use the Dow-Jones Commodity Average, the Associated Press Average, or any of several other statistical attempts to build a model of the whole market. Relating commodity contracts to the Dow-Jones Commodity Average, and using the same plus-one-for-better-performance, minus-one-for-worse-action technique, it was found that momentum-moti-

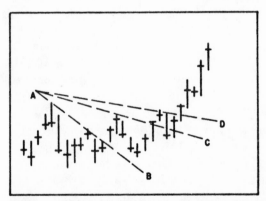

Figure 4   *This is a fanline breakout. When three increasingly flatter trendlines can be drawn connecting the same top to a series of three lower tops, breakout from within the fanlines is interpreted by many commodity chart analysts as indication of a new movement beginning.*

vated transactions in three commodities totaling ten trades during the year gave an overall theoretical profit of $7,297.50. This worked out to be seven profit trades totaling $8,641.90 and three at losses running to $1,344.40. The average profit from all ten trades was $729.75.

If you are a stock trader who has been watching charts for years, you will have noted by now that not all of the old relia-bles of the boardroom have been mentioned here. The reason is that commodity chart analysis, our study showed, has im-portant differences from charting applied to stocks, and those differences tend to make some things more useful as commod-ity timing tools than they are in the stock market, while some of them work less well.

With stocks, bonds, preferreds, and all the other merchandise of Wall Street; there are finite numbers of certificates. If 200 mil-lion shares exist and his best studies convince him that 150 million of these are closely held in family or institutional hands, a stock market trader or investor knows that a certain volume of trading can "eat through" the part of the remaining 50 million shares which are outstanding floating, and that when this is done there won't be any more shares for sale at the prices around which the action had been gyrating. If peo-ple still want the stock, they will have to bid higher. Ergo: Its price should rise.

But in commodities there are infinite numbers of futures contracts—thus no amount of trading can be said with confi-dence to have eaten through the supply. Therefore the same methods don't always work (although many do work well), and some of those that work will be found to require slightly new rules for operating. It is like putting an automobile driver behind the wheel of a boat. Actions such as swinging the wheel will produce the same results, but he has to accus-tom himself to the *feel* of a new vehicle.

The rationale which underlies timing study states that the prices of a free market thing are produced out of the melting pot decisions of the well-informed and the ill-informed, the rich and the poor, the steady and the scared. A tenet of this rationale states that the rich are more likely to be well in-formed than otherwise, since poor information is not conducive to the building or keeping of fat bank statements and that their heavier battalions of capital will eventually prevail.

TO RECAP:

1. Such things as soybeans, hog bellies, plywood, and palladium, lumped collectively as commodities, do not sound very glamorous or interesting. But they represent one of the fastest of the Roads to Wealth.

2. Commodity futures contracts exist primarily to protect producers and users of commodities from the vagaries of the pricing machinery by pegging down a present price for future use. The risk they seek to avoid must, however, be put on someone's shoulders. And so the speculator—in this case, you, as a seeker of fast wealth—enters. He assumes the risk in hope of reaping a profit from the price changes and fluctuations which both user and producer of commodities seek to avoid.

3. A commodities contract is an intangible. Profits are made (and often, for inept speculators, lost) by trading the contract while not owning or having to deliver the actual goods.

4. Great leverage exists in a commodities contract. The margin required to swing metals, eggs, grains, granulated sugar, etc., is usually about 10 percent of the actual value. The result is that a very small move of 10 percent in actual price can represent a doubling of invested capital, or, if the move goes against a trader, a wiping out of the amount put into the situation.

5. It therefore becomes important not to plunge, but always to hold back a reserve in the knowledge that until perfection becomes possible in human beings, errors of judgment will continue to plague speculators as well as car drivers, skin divers, bankers, and bakers.

6. Commodities are volatile. Where a swinging stock could

bring about a doubling (or a halving) in invested capital in a six-month period, a swinging commodity contract might do the same thing in six days—or less.

7. Important, too, is the possession of all vital facts. The first kind of factual study involves such things as the economic situation; the problems and prospects of foreign trade; the demand and production facts about a number of different commodities, competition, and current news.

8. Many commodity speculators say that the technical facts are as important and some claim that they are more important than the fundamental background facts. Timing via technical study is usually done by means of charts. Chart study is not infallible, but experience shows that it often gives early notice when a change of price direction change has taken place.

9

The Franchising Bit

A GOOD WAY to begin reading this chapter on the most vital new development in business—that's franchising, suh, as the Kentucky Colonel might say—would be to go back and briefly skim over the parts of Chapter One which described George's adventure in steak-with-clam-juice land.

George's adventures were certainly no more fantastic than the real life franchising saga of Kentucky Fried Chicken, cooked with a secret recipe to produce "finger-lickin' goodness." Kentucky Fried Chicken was built from a small beginning by a man, and later an organization, whose genesis was a country service station which dispensed food on the side to hungry travelers.

It was started by Harland Sanders, the famous colonel

whose goatee, string tie, and other accouterments have become as familiar to television watchers as his homey wisdom. Beginning in 1930, he sold chicken to travelers stopping at his station in Corbin, Kentucky. The franchised operation was begun in 1955.

In 1964, the colonel sold out for $2 million plus a lifetime job as sales representative, corporate image, and household god of the operation. (In the latter capacity, the eighty-year-old Sanders has recently been grooming a nephew who resembles him to take over some of his public appearance chores.)

Kentucky Fried Chicken had grown, by 1955, to a modest-sized chain of franchised "stores." Under new management since 1964, the number of units has proliferated, the stock has been listed on the New York Stock Exchange, and the total value of Kentucky Fried Chicken has become half a billion dollars. The company is currently reaching out to start a chain of motels—franchised, of course.

It has been quite a trek out of the Kentucky hills to that kind of affluence. The franchising road is probably the only one which could have led the little service station sideline so far.

Franchising is no longer a baby, but one of the biggest business operations around, and, by all odds, the fastest-growing despite its already hefty size. According to *The Franchise Business,* a small business advisory pamphlet published by the Bank of America, "Franchising is well over a $60 billion industry, contributing a healthy 10% of the Gross National Product."

Just what *is* franchising? The Bank of America's definition is one of the best offered for this mighty phenomenon:

> Franchising is a chain of small businesses bound by the image and policies of a parent company. The person buying a franchise (the franchisee) does not buy his own business. He buys a success package from a company (the franchisor) who shows him how to use it.

In a way, the franchisee cannot be his own boss because he may be risking the franchisor's money or reputation. This is one reason the franchisor closely supervises its franchises. Actually, the franchise agreement approaches the concept of a partnership with the franchisee becoming a junior partner . . . a good franchise provides a beneficial relationship to both parties and abuses neither party.

There is no one way all franchise operations work. The Bank of America's franchise study broke them down this way:

Territorial or Area Franchise—The sales area is usually large enough to warrant sub-franchising, and the franchisee's responsibility is to develop outlets within his territory. He can often operate an outlet and receive additional income from the franchises he establishes.

Operating Franchise—The franchisee operates his own franchise or several franchises, but he does not sub-franchise. This type of franchise takes several forms.

Co-ownership Franchise—The franchisor and the franchisee usually become 50-50 partners. Both own half the business and split the profits.

Co-managership Franchise—The franchisee buys a managerial interest in the business. The franchisor owns the building and the equipment but does not share the profits according to his investment. He usually receives a lesser amount such as a percent of gross sales.

Lease Franchise—This is much like the co-managership franchise except the franchisor does not share the profits of the business. The franchisee buys a lease to operate the business and has little or no investment in the business fixtures. The franchisor makes his profit on the lease and the merchandise sold to the franchisee.

Licensee Franchise—The franchisor supplies the methods and merchandise for operating the business, but the franchisee usually buys or rents the building and furnishes it with the approval of the franchisor. The franchisor receives a percentage of gross sales.

Manufacturing Franchise—The franchisor supplies manufacturing knowledge, patterns, molds, and materials for completion and sale of the product. This is similar to a licensee franchise.

Distributorship Franchise—The franchisee handles the local warehousing and regional sales of merchandise for several manufacturers (franchisors) because of geographical inconvenience or shipping problems. Many merchants are exclusive distributors for lines of clothing, sporting goods, food, tools, and other items.

The structural mechanics of franchising—the kind of relationships, contracts, selling, buying, manufacturing, and servicing setups—is wide. Wider still is the variety of merchandise and service being franchised.

There are the fast food franchise operations like Kentucky Fried Chicken; Roy Rogers Roast Beef; fish 'n' puppies; fish 'n' chips; hot dogs by dozens of brand names; hamburger heavens; Italian specialty palazzos; ice cream, both soft and hard; sizzling steakeries; country cookin' counters; taco take-outs; pizza emporiums; haciendas for lovers of hot Mexican fare; cheese chalets. By comparison with some of these fast food operations, George's Clam Juice Steak Houses seem not only feasible, but actually conservative in concept.

Food operations are not all there is to the franchise business. Looking over a few days' ads in one idea source alone—"The Mart" classified section of the daily *Wall Street Journal*—shows such operations offered to prospective franchisees as:

Corrective reading institutes; auto wash shops; management consulting services for small business, and presumably for big business as well should any high-powered executives apply; a service to search out inventors for people who want to back new ideas which are as yet unhatched; one to wed acquisition and merger partners and even serve up advice to the corporate lovelorn who are searching for merger partners; a full-fledged franchised business college operation; retail electronics shops; transportation service for handicapped children and adults; a chain of art galleries, no less; other chains of boutiques, shops, stores, and specialty places to dish up clothing for all the family; a gift-by-phone network.

Other days' financial advertising for franchises indicated existence of franchised tiling contractorships; mobile homes centers; success motivation distributorships; computer schools and computerized data processing centers; security systems to guard plants, stores, shopping centers, homes; golf courses; photo shops with a supermarket twist; photocopying centers; campgrounds; one which offers to help others use dollar leverage in exciting, innovative, and highly profitable ways; transmission shops, muffler shops, and other places where sick automobiles are rejuvenated; motor inns; temporary help suppliers, some furnishing office girls, some plant workers, some specialized people such as medical technicians; leasing and rental stores; pet shops, brick shops, bakery shops, food shops; tax consultants, marketing consultants, travel consultants, advertising consultants; schools to handle automated learning, medical and dental assistantship training.

The *Franchises Annual,* a book put out by National Franchise Reports, lists eighty-two classifications of franchised business in its 1969 issue.

If you are seeking big money, you should be aware on which side the sizable sums are made. *Franchisees* are the people who buy franchises. They usually make a good living, often better than they would be able to make with comparable capital and training if they went it alone. *Franchisors* are the people who sell franchises to franchisees. They are the people who make the big money and who are more likely to find franchising a Road to Wealth, as distinguished from mere monetary sufficiency.

Keep that in mind throughout the discussion to follow. We're taking the franchise road as *franchisors.*

However, it is axiomatic in business and in most of the rest of life that if a deal is going to be a good one and is going to last, then both parties to the deal should find it profitable. With that in mind, let us look at some of the advantages and the pitfalls that await both parties.

To quote from the study made by the Bank of America:

The advantages of franchising to the franchisor have been summed up as follows:
1. Investment capital for expansion.
2. Interested local management with cost and sales awareness.
3. Acceptance as a local establishment in the community.
4. Limited payroll and insurance costs.
5. Better marketing communications.
6. Good motivation resulting from individual ownership.
7. Thorough and selective distribution.
8. Elimination of selling costs, thus reducing operating expenses.

These advantages are partially offset by supervisory costs. The franchisor also loses some control of the operation because franchisees are more independent than managers, making it more difficult to maintain a standardized operation, regulate sales promotions, and rely on a feedback of information. Franchisees often want to add a product to the already established line of merchandise, make their purchases from other sources than those specified by the parent company, plan their own promotions, and often neglect monthly reports.

To the franchisee go the benefits of the franchisor's knowledge. His parent company smooths the rough edges of a small business by eliminating two prime causes of failure—under-capitalization and lack of business knowhow. In addition, the franchisor places more resources in the hands of the franchisee than he could ever hope to command himself. A well-organized, well-controlled franchise system offers the franchisee:
1. A chance to open a business without previous experience.
2. A chance to open a business with less capital.
3. Adequate financial assistance.
4. A consumer-accepted image.
5. Maintained quality.
6. Combined buying power allowing purchase advantages.
7. Basic training and continued assistance.
8. Location analysis.
9. Financial capability to buy choice locations.
10. Advantageous rental or leasing rates.
11. Well-designed facilities, fixtures, displays, supplies.
12. Managerial and records assistance.

13. Sales, advertising, and marketing assistance.
14. National publicity, promotion, and recognition.
15. Higher income potential.
16. Lower risk of failure.
17. Continual research and development.

These benefits are not free. The franchisee pays for them in various ways. For example, the franchisee usually agrees to pay the parent company money in addition to the flat cost of the franchise. This sum may be a percent of gross sales, a flat fee each year, or a markup on supplies, rent, or initial equipment.

The franchisee must also accept a certain amount of standardization and control he would not otherwise have if he were completely independent. Nevertheless, the benefits far outweigh the failings of franchising for both the franchisor and the franchisee. This is evidenced by the growing number of people and businesses interested in making the franchise system work for them.

In this interchange of advantages and disadvantages the franchisor—that's you—obtains tremendous leverage. He has working for him the capital the franchisee has invested in his store or office, since a percentage of the profit results reaped by that capital usually accrues to him. In addition, he has the sweat and time of the franchisee to give him personal leverage.

The franchisee, too, has leverage. He has the skill, experience, and profit-minded supervision of the franchisor to leverage his own efforts. In money matters, he often has bank credit available to him (none, of course, if he is a bad credit risk) for swinging construction, etc. Sometimes, franchisee financing is done through the help of the franchisor, and on occasion borrowing is in the name of the franchisor but secured by the franchised property. Experience has shown that franchisees often make 15 to 18 percent on their sales volume. On occasion they clear 20 percent and even 25 percent.

That is what you might make being a *franchisee*. How do *franchisors* fare? With the need to sometimes help the franchisee along, does the franchisor need a big bankroll to start in business?

Al Lapin didn't. In eleven years, he parlayed a $25,000 investment, not all his own but some borrowed and some invested by others, into a business whose assets the investment house of Merrill Lynch, Pierce, Fenner & Smith estimated at $120 million.

In its July 23, 1969, issue of *Investor's Reader,* Merrill Lynch reported on this amazing tale of growth into big wealth through franchising:

International Industries is a major contender in the franchise industry. Corporate revenues are running around $60,000,000 for fiscal 1969 which ends next month; total retail volume by all the franchised plus the few directly operated units adds to about $25,000,000. When it comes to breadth, International may well be No. 1 with 14 different franchise operations. Its franchisees sell pancakes, pies, ice cream or dresses, teach secretaries or paramedical personnel, collect unpaid bills, rent medical equipment.

It all started when Lapin was 31. He had . . . a coffee catering business in Los Angeles. The success of the latter motivated him towards restaurants and the first International House of Pancakes opened in Burbank in July 1958. The $25,000 investment came from Al, his father . . . his brother Jerry (who has left the company) and three silent partners.

Success came soon. "We sold the first franchise in 1959 and they really began to roll in about 1961, the year we went public. We went on the Amex in 1964 and to the Big Board in April 1968." Al Lapin is proud "we are among a handful of companies that have made it to the Big Board in less than ten years."

International House of Pancakes was the corporate title until 1963 and pancakes are still the biggest revenue producer with 241 Houses in 34 states. But every year INT goes further afield taking advantage of franchise opportunities. Lapin relates, "I felt since we had mastered restaurants we were in an excellent position to try franchising other things. Restaurants are much harder to supervise than other retail operations so the sledding was downhill. A successful franchisor does not sell hamburgers or chicken, he sells a business system. The franchise method of distribution can be applied to most any retail business consis-

tent with its size—not too big for an unsophisticated businessman but not so small he's just buying a job."

Today Lapin's company, now known as International Industries, operates in fourteen—count 'em—franchise fields.

From Minnie Pearl to political power might be the capsul-
ized story of John Jay Hooker, head of Performance Systems
and currently (as this is written) a candidate for Governor of
Tennessee.

Beginning small in Nashville, Minnie Pearl (corporate
name now changed to Performance Systems) built a suddenly
successful chain of fast food restaurants across the country.
Many who backed the venture in Nashville in its early days,
investing thousands, were worth millions in a few years.

Earl Gagosian invested $5,000 of his own and borrowed
$50,000 (thus beginning with heavy leverage) to set up Royal
Inns. That was in 1965. Four years later, his personal worth
was well up in the millions of dollars. In its August 5, 1969,
issue, *California Financial Journal* reported on Gagosian's fantastic Horatio Alger franchising story:

> Royal Inns' program is co-ownership of each unit, usually
> with the operator as partner. For Canada, Hawaii and Mexico,
> a franchise program is under way. Gagosian figures the com-
> pany can expand either or both ways.
> "We have a goal of 300 inns by 1975 and we're on schedule,"
> Gagosian said. "How did I do it? I put $5,000 into Royal Inns
> stock, that's all. Today it is worth more than $12 million on its
> own."
> Spreading out from San Diego, the chain is now over-spread-
> ing the country, chiefly in the West and South, and on into
> Canada and Mexico. The first Inn went up in 1965 in Palm
> Springs; today there are 21. Hilton and Holiday Inns may have
> to make room at the top for the 46-year-old carpenter from
> Southern California. "I've got a few more million dollars in
> mind," he confessed, smiling.

By far the greatest number of franchising operations revolve
around fast food. You can buy any of a dozen kinds of fried

chicken. You can buy chicken with dirty rice, chicken with
clean rice, chicken without any rice, chicken barbecued, fried,
sautéed, broiled, or with anything else done to it. You can buy
plain hamburgers, giant hamburgers, super-giant hamburgers,
whoppers, super-extra-duper-big hamburgers. You can buy
your burger in a den, hamlet, or chef's palace. If your taste
runs to beef, you can satisfy it with spare ribs, roast beef sandwiches, beefburgers, beefsteaks, both sir and otherwise. Want
a good old American hot dog? There are plain dogs, hot dogs
with beer on the side, hot dogs cooked in beer. If it's seafood
you want, franchised stores offer fish, fishburgers, and fish and
chips; Italian food ranges from pizza under a variety of names
but still pizza, to spaghetti. There are Yum Yum restaurants
and Zum Zum restaurants.

"So for gosh sakes, if you want to go into franchising, *don't*
dream up another kind of eatery," pleaded one franchising
consultant with whom I discussed this.

> I know towns where there are as many as three fried chicken
> places under as many names in a two-block area of one
> busy street, with a couple of other branded chicken houses on a
> thoroughfare only a few blocks away. In between, all kinds of
> other franchised stores cater to the eating-out habit. So stay
> away from franchising foods unless you have a new twist—such
> as that steak with clam juice idea I heard from a fellow named
> George.

However, another angle on fast-food overcrowding was offered by a second franchising expert from Chicago with whom
I discussed the question.

"Overcrowded? Bosh!" he said.

> There is an old axiom of gasoline selling that says if you
> want to make a service station successful, set it up where there
> are other stations because the two or three stations together
> will pull more than two or three times the traffic that a single
> station might be expected to bring. It is that way in food retail-

ing. *But* (and this is a matter where I believe many franchisors of food fall down) it is important to question whether your structure is right for the sales volume. More fast-food franchises fail because of this problem than because of alleged overcrowding.

For example: The rule of thumb in this field says occupancy costs should not exceed 8 percent of volume. Recently, I was called in to consider plans for a series of buildings costing about $500,000 each. I told the franchisor he would go broke with such buildings. The reason was that his average food ticket was about 50 cents. Put the building on a fifteen-year depreciation table. That gives yearly occupancy cost of $33,333.33. You have to have an annual volume at that figure of $416,-667.00. Break it down further and it comes to $34,722.92 a month. This store would have an average check of 50 cents, the owner told me, and in turn that would mean 69,446 customers had to be served each month. He planned to open six days a week because of laws in some states. So with twenty-six days a month of operation, 2,671 customers a day were required. His $500,000 restaurants just weren't designed to handle the crowd. Better to design less costly buildings, I told him, or else find some expensive items to sell. The arithmetic of building cost is more important than the arithmetic of how many competitors there will be.

Both of these opinions were proffered by experts. But food service, fast or otherwise, is not your only choice. The range of franchising ideas is as wide as the broad spectrum of American industry and services. A number of good ideas might be gleaned from a useful book put out by the U.S. Department of Commerce called *Growth Pace Setters in American Industry, 1958–1968*. It lists the areas which enjoyed fastest growth in the decade and gives tables and descriptions of each.

While it might not be entirely wise to set up a chain of franchised blast furnaces, paper mills, or petroleum refineries —three of the pace-setting growth areas—the book offers many ideas. Successful franchise chains have already been developed in computer technology and services, selling electronic gear, motor vehicle parts and services, photographic equipment and servicing, dental equipment and supplies, and others of the listed fast-growth field.

The complete USDC list of pace-setting growth industries of 1958–1968 follows:

Aircraft; automatic vending machines; blast furnaces and steel mills; boat-building; book publishing and printing; cathode ray picture tubes; commercial printing, lithographic; computing and related machines; construction machinery; corrugated and solid fiber boxes; dental equipment and supplies; electrical housewares and fans; elevators and moving stairways; farm machinery; fiber cans, tubes and drums; frozen fruits, juices and vegetables; industrial gas cleaning equipment; industrial process controls, industrial trucks and tractors; jewelry, precious metal; knit fabrics; manifold business forms; manmade fibers, noncellulosic; meat packing; mechanical measuring devices; metal-cutting machine tools; metal office furniture; motor vehicles and parts; newspapers; optical instruments and lenses; organic chemicals; paper mills; petroleum refining; pharmaceutical preparations; photographic equipment; plastics materials and resins; plastic products; primary aluminum; radio communications equipment; radio and television receiving sets; railroad cars; refrigeration machinery; semiconductors; special dies and tools, steel foundries; surgical and medical instruments; synthetic rubber; telephone and telegraph apparatus; textile machinery; toilet preparations; toys and games; trailer coaches; truck and bus bodies; truck trailers; tufted carpets and rugs.

An impractical list for franchising? Not if you apply the methods of "creativity" to the list and think of what relates to each of these. To tie in with the growth of frozen foods, you need not set up franchised plants. A chain of stores specializing in gourmet frozen foods could be highly successful. Manifold business forms take heavy equipment to manufacture but not to retail, and a franchise catering to the paperwork needs of small business might be a winner. Industrial trucks and tractors are big stuff. But it takes no more to inventory a specialized kind of equipment catering to specialized markets than it would to set up a fried chicken chain. Each of the USDC growth industry ideas could trigger a related franchising idea.

"My advice would be to seek something unusual," says Richard M. Farver, area director for Continental Franchise Corp.

> An example is the successful operation to register pets. It is called American Dog Registry, and appeals to millions of dog owners everywhere. At a conservative estimate of the dog population in an average area, the potential is staggering. This franchise offers to tattoo an owner's Social Security number onto the dog's underside. Then if the dog is lost, the registry checks SPCA's, police and fire departments, hospitals (which sometimes buy strays for lab work), etc. It makes thievery unprofitable and is tremendously successful. Just a simple idea—but what potential!

Rick Farver cites another service which is removed from the general run of franchise ideas, but is sound in concept and likely to succeed. "That's an employment and placement service specializing in salesman," he says.

> Not route salesmen or necktie salesmen, but salesmen up in the bigger-income brackets. The franchisees work together in that Company A might need an executive salesman in Minnesota, and find him through a franchise outlet in Georgia. Fees are paid by the hiring firm, no charge to the salesman, and the bracket of salesman is high enough to make sizable finding fees possible. Different—you bet. But good.

There is not, it would appear, any one "right" idea certain to produce a profitable franchise. As Al Lapin pointed out, a successful franchisor is not so much a merchant of transmissions, chickens, or drugs as a seller of business systems. Apply the right system in the right way, and most of the potential services or merchandise areas you might choose become the "right" ones for you. But you can't just begin peddling franchise contracts. You must first establish a pilot.

A pilot operation, in franchising, is a place in which you actually do the franchising thing you have determined upon. As George did with his Clam Juice Steak Houses and with George's Fast Food Computer, the pilot serves to determine whether the franchising idea is a workable one or one which merely looks good. Moreover—if and when it is successful—it serves as a shining example toward which you can point proudly when talking to franchisee prospects, and whose dollars and cents figures you can cite as achievable possibilities, not merely wishful thinking.

The pilot is your proving ground and your showcase.

After it has been successful as a proving ground, you have a decision to make. You can either take your franchising plans and problems to a franchising service organization or you can do the franchisee selling yourself.

These service organizations' names are to be found in advertisements on newspapers' financial pages where franchise opportunities are advertised. The companies perform a useful service—at a fee, of course—and can, for their fee, relieve you of the problems of selling and even of servicing your franchisees. Not least, the better firms give sound advice on the saleability of a franchising idea and can suggest ways to make a mediocre package a real Road to Wealth.

Here is the way one such organization describes the package it can offer franchisors:

> We will advise, consult and help you set up your franchise program. Provide answers to such questions as: How much is an adequate and fair franchise fee—royalty and package price? What are our needs for working capital and franchisee financing? How many franchises can we expect to sell each year and in total—based on the optimum rate of expansion? What will our cost be over the first five years of the program and what return can be anticipated on our investment of manpower and money? How do we provide for continuing profitable operation after the burst of new sales is over? How do we assure success for our franchisees?

We will also act as the franchising arm of your corporation, set up and operate programs based on correct answers to questions like these: What type, if any, pilot operation is required —how is it set up, operated and evaluated? How is a franchise recruiting program launched? Who, how many and what type of person is needed for implementation? How is the franchise program operated to take advantage of existing profit making factors?

We can take over the total management function of any franchisor, or supplement your executive and operating personnel in a franchise operation on whatever level you desire . . . develop prototype operations to prove operating methods and validate results . . . provide franchisor sales training programs . . . provide franchisee management and operational training programs.

But many franchisors prefer to handle operations on their own. If you plan to go alone, place this list of franchise marketers' services on the wall and stare hard at it every day. These steps constitute franchise selling.

You will need to give your franchise a name. Many new operations carry the names of show business figures and big stars from pro football, golf, and baseball. It may be true or not that when the public enters one of Broadway Joe's restaurants it expects to see Joe Namath, Jets uniform and all, behind the counter, or that it figures Mickey Mantle as the country cook of Mickey Mantle's Country Cookin'. But it's certain that the big name attracts big crowds, at least initially.

But say that you have decided to sell your idea for a chain of clam juice-flavored steak houses across the country, and may have determined that it will go under the name of George's Clam Juice Steak Houses, since Minnie Pearl, Johnny Carson, Dizzy Dean, Ed McMahon, Joe Namath, Mickey Mantle, Rowan and Martin, and a few other big-pull national names are already spoken for.

You plan the advertising or go to an advertising agency to do planning for you. Time passes. The advertisements run. Applications flood in. If you are smart, you'll probably reject more than you accept because no franchise applicant should be considered (remembering that you're risking the good name of George's Clam Juice Steak Houses every time an unknown operator opens an emporium under that name) without finding out several things:

■ Has he the money to swing the deal? Sufficient capital merely to pay the franchise fee and hold inventory isn't enough. Every business needs working funds, and this is especially true of a new business in its first months.

■ What is his character? A man with a past record of shady operation or one who brings out a distasteful reaction in fellow businessmen isn't likely to enhance either the reputation or bank account of George's Clam Juice Steak Houses.

■ What is his background? Insufficient education should bar anyone from consideration. However, sufficient doesn't mean Ph.D. honors or even possession of a baccalaureate—or attendance at college for that matter. Business background counts too.

■ How does his personality come over in close contact? Whether the product is orange juice or outer space hardware, a franchisee has to *sell* it. Many franchisors employ psychological tests to determine aptitude for selling as well as for sizzling George's Clam Juice Steaks.

■ Is he a team man? The loner will go off to form his own steak house corporation, possibly using tomato juice and vodka and calling it Bill's Bloody Mary Steak Boutique. Franchising is essentially a team operation. The team members—franchisees—have to be people who participate.

If a franchisee is smart he, too, is going to ask a number of questions, and George had better be ready to bat them when they come. The U.S. Small Business Administration has a booklet called *Are You Ready for Franchising?* It was authored by A. L. Tunick who is president of Chicken Delight, Inc., and charter president of the International Franchise Association. Mr. Tunick suggests that local businessmen ask a number of questions before they sign a franchisor's contract:

—Is there a franchise fee? If so, what is the basis for it?

—Are there continuing royalties?

—What is the total cash investment required and what are the terms for financing the balance?

—Does the cash investment include payment for fixtures and equipment?

—How do prices for fixtures and equipment compare with competitive prices in the open market?

—Will you be required to participate in company-sponsored promotion and publicity by contributing a percentage of profits to an "advertising fund"? If so, will you have the right to veto any increase in contributions to the fund?

—If the parent company's product or service is protected by patent or liability insurance, is the same protection extended to you?

—Under what conditions may your franchise be cancelled?

—What special form of continuing assistance does the company obligate itself to give you after you are operating the business?

—Under what terms may you sell the business to whomever you please at whatever price you may be able to obtain?

—Will you be compelled to sell any new products introduced by the parent company after you have opened the business?

—How can you terminate your agreement if you are not happy for some reason?

—In essence, does the course you want to take parallel that of the franchisor? Does his success depend on your success?

TO RECAP:

1. Horatio Alger's heroes went from rags to riches by hard work. Hard work is still an ingredient, but many people today are going via another road—franchising. Success stories such as that of Kentucky Fried Chicken spur them along.

2. Franchising is a system by which the franchisor (the fel-

low who operates the parent company) utilizes two kinds of leverage. The money of the franchisee (the man who owns the store on the corner of Podunk and Unreal and sells the franchisor's products) is employed for both parties. The time and skill of the franchisee is likewise at work for the franchisor, lending to franchising a kind of leverage not found elsewhere.

3. But the franchisee is not a serf. Leverage works its way too. The successful methods and the proven products or services pushed by the franchisor are his to use, saving for him many of the uncertainties of owning one's own business and earning for him a rate of return on capital and sales usually greater than those of other inexperienced small businessmen.

4. There are many different franchising formats. Franchising has been able to fit everything from fried chicken to computer training, transmissions to tax service.

5. Some amazing tales have been recorded of franchisors' successes from small beginnings to sudden affluence. One ran a $25,000 investment into a $120-million-assets corporation in eleven years.

6. If you want to be a franchisor, determine what you will sell, then set up a pilot operation as proving ground and showcase.

7. Then decide whether to sell through a franchise marketing service, which might both package and sell your deal, or set up your own sales organization.

8. Many franchisors say you will stand or fall by the caliber of the franchisees you accept. It therefore becomes important to grade, cull, and pick these with care.

10

The Merger Money Machine

WE HAVE TREATED EXTENSIVELY in this book the story, characters, plot, and circumstances of that glorious adventure entitled "George's Clam Juice Steak Houses." Now we are going to look at how it grew after franchising by applying double leverage atop the borrowed money which got George started and how the whole thing became a vast money machine.

Move the scene to a day when, after expanding via franchise to become a national restaurateur, and then successfully launching a second venture, itself franchised, known as George's Fast Food Computer, George—a bit portlier in physical girth and a good deal wealthier in the pocketbook department—sat down to a luncheon of clam juice-flavored steak with his CPA to discuss going public in order to provide for the companies' continuation after his retirement and to establish a market value for his holdings.

In this chapter we will discuss the *desirability* of going public versus its possible drawbacks. Since it is, most times, a necessary beginning step to travel on the merry merger route to wealth, and since George used his stock acquired through going public to go on to further success instead of retiring, let's examine here what going public means.

When you "go public," you cease to be a private person named George and become an institution. You sell some of your ownership of George's Clam Juice Steak Houses to the public in the form of stock. Sometimes, this involves turning a privately owned company, a joint venture, or partnership, into a corporation. A lawyer can do that for you in a twinkling. If you are already incorporated, but only a few people hold stock, you have a nonpublic corporation. To turn this into a public corporation takes something more than a twinkling. When the changeover has been made, you are likely to find that the value of your personal wealth is no longer measurable in buildings, land, or restaurant tables for which there is no immediate market, but in publicly traded stock for which there is. Most of all, you will have acquired the necessary base for proceeding with merger and acquisition growth because you will have created the tender, nearly as legal as dollar bills and in many cases more useful, with which to merge and acquire.

Going public involves parting with a portion of your equity and receiving for it cold, hard personal cash. This is likely to be greater than sale of the equivalent amount of land, buildings, or restaurant tables would have brought in. If you are smart, and well advised by an underwriter adept at his trade of planning packages to go public and then marketing them, you will have held back a controlling interest. With mergers on your mind, you will have moreover planned so that the treasury of the new public corporation will possess enough stock or be empowered to issue enough convertible debentures, convertible preferreds, and/or warrants to give it a big buying power of the kind that, in the right hands and at the right times, have brought some entrepreneurs like you and George to sudden, sizable wealth.

A look at the regulatory steps involved in going public frightens many merger-minded people. But it need not be as difficult as it looks. If you sell only to residents within your state, you can take the sometimes shorter cut of an intrastate offering. A small interstate offering can be done through the SEC on short forms and with less folderol than a big offering requires.

But this chapter is not a primer on the mechanics of going public. To accomplish this, you will need the help of a good lawyer, a good, tax-smart accountant standing at his shoulder, and—sometimes overseeing, sometimes advising both of them —a sound, ethical and sales-oriented new issue underwriter.

So back, for now, to George's Clam Juice Steak Houses and George's Fast Food Computer.

Armed with his merger money, George, instead of retiring as he had planned, began to cast covetous glances about him. "That's a nice dry cleaning establishment on the other side of town," he told Ronnie one morning as they sipped coffee and discussed the business outlook. "The cleaning people have an interesting idea in their fifteen-minute service, and I believe it could be made into as big a thing as the Clam Juice Steak Houses. Suppose we make 'em an offer."

"Five thousand shares, worth $12.50 a share on the open market—that is what I will give you for the business," said George the next week in an interview with the dry cleaner.

"It is a steal, George, at that price," the prospect answered, "but I won't deny that I'd be interested in selling out if the price were right. Some nice, publicly traded stock that looks to be worth more in the future than it is now would be just the thing. Say ten thousand shares?"

Out of this discussion, supplemented with several martinis and a dinner of clam juice-flavored steak at the nearest George's store, the deal was made firm for eight thousand shares which, the market being at the time a good one, had climbed to $13.62 a share at the time the sale went through.

Now George owned a third business. Some of the cash received from going public went to spruce it up and start it on the way to becoming the pilot of George's Fast Cleaning chain of franchised outlets. George looked about some more and saw a machine shop in the next state. Its attraction was a backlog of Air Force orders. George approached the owner. A sale was consummated for $100,000 in 4 percent bonds, carrying a conversion feature which allowed the machine shop owner to change them into common stock at $20 per share.

"See?" said George when he and Ronnie next met. "Now I'm on my way to becoming a conglomerate. I have a lot of other strings to my bow. *And the beauty of it all is that this merger route calls for no extra money—just stock, convertibles, and warrants.*"

The merger road is a wide one. Corporations of vast size grew to be what they are now by playing the merger game. But it is not a game for big boys alone. You can play it, as Al Lapin played it with borrowed money, as Earl Gagosian played it with moderate amounts of money, mostly borrowed. These men applied their borrowed money leverage to both franchising and to merger acquisition. Others apply it to manufacturing and merger, to service industries and acquisition merger. The key thing we're discussing in this chapter is not so much the business with which you begin as the techniques of merger and acquisition which you use to make it a big business.

According to statistics released by W. T. Grimm and Co.

and reported in late September, 1969, during the first nine months of 1969 alone there were 4,217 consolidations—34 percent more than the same period of 1968. Not all of them were the mergers of big corporations with other big corporations. Some were fellows starting small with the intention of growing big via mergers and acquisitions. Before proceeding, it might be well to define mergers and acquisitions. The Center for Study of Democratic Institutions, an independent, nonprofit institution, recently published a study called *The Conglomerate Corporation,* authored by Neil H. Jacoby, professor in the Graduate School of Business Administration of UCLA. Wrote Dr. Jacoby in explanation of the merger process:

Modes of enterprise expansion may be classified as follows:
(1) Vertical
    (a) Backward (toward raw material sources)
    (b) Forward (toward consumers of final products)
(2) Horizontal (market extension within the same industry)
(3) Product extension (into additional industries)
    (a) Producing related products (concentric)
    (b) Producing unrelated products (conglomerate)

Merger is a minor method of growth of American business corporations, the predominant source being internally generated funds. Up to recent years most mergers have been of the vertical or horizontal types, in which the surviving firms acquired other firms within the same industries or industrial groups. During the nineteen-sixties, however, most large mergers involved firms operating in different industries. Some encompassed firms producing products that were related with respect to sources of raw materials, production technology, or marketing channels. These have been aptly termed "concentric" companies. Others involved unrelated enterprises—the true conglomerates.

Thus many mergers are between unrelated businesses. Many are as diverse as the merger of George's Clam Juice Steak Houses with a dry cleaning establishment and later with a machine shop.

Can anybody run such widespread activities efficiently?

Royal Little has been called the granddad of the conglomerate idea of merging and acquiring businesses that seem to bear no relation to each other. In an interview in *Dun's Review,* May, 1968, he said:

> It has now been shown that through the combination of normal internal growth, plus growth through unrelated business acquisitions, you can get a better cumulative growth rate on capital than can be obtained in any normal, single industry operation. That, I believe, is why unrelated diversification is here to stay, because you just can't beat it unless you're the one in a hundred thousand that comes up with a Xerox or Polaroid. *Unrelated diversification will beat any normal single-industry company when it comes to return on net worth and cumulative growth rate of earnings per share of common stock.* [Italics supplied.]

It is well to know, however, that merger-minded corporations are not immune from the law which says what any organization from a mammal, bird, or fish to a giant impersonal corporation tends to have a cycle of growth, maturity, then senescence. You can whoop it up mightily in the early days of a merger-slanted growth policy and when you have grown to maturity still put on wealth-building fireworks. The old-age stage may be a long way off. Don't worry about it in your growth days.

In those young days when a merger policy is beginning to show sharp growth, you should be aware that the potential targets aren't confined to businesses smaller than your own. In the Bible, David slew Goliath. In the business world of today, he sometimes eats Goliath whole.

Going public is not the only way to get your hands on stock and other securities for purchasing possible acquisitions. There is another, quicker way. In some cases people with only a small stake rattling around in their bank accounts have been successful in building instant corporate empires by utilizing this method.

It is called the "shell game."

In the hands of an unscrupulous operator, the shell game in business is not very distinguishable from the three-card monte known by that name in carnivals and in street corner gambling gyps. That this has occasionally been used in crooked ways, however, is not an indictment of the shell game *in toto*.

It goes this way:

Inspired by George's success in building first a chain of clam juice-flavored steak houses and then in using those for further leverage to expand, Ronnie approached a broker in New York City. "I want to go into merger expansion, too," he told the broker. "What's the quickest way for a man with a modest stake?"

"Buy a shell," answered the broker.

A corporate shell, this broker explained, is much like the shell of a hermit crab from which the living organism has departed. The shell is still there although it no longer moves or serves as a home.

"Here is one shell," the broker continued. "A company that made automotive accessories. The assets and operations were sold off a year ago. The name exists, the stock is still outstanding, although the stockholders have long ago been paid their shares of money and securities received in the sale of assets. It is a corporate shell with nothing inside. Interested? I believe I can obtain control for you for a few thousand."

Soon the proud possessor of a shell corporation whose name he immediately changed to Rontronics, Ronnie commenced operation. He cast an eye on a small intrastate railroad which was possessed of three locomotives, a half dozen cars, and just enough business to keep it from degenerating to the level of the Cannonball Express. Ronnie made an offer of 100,000 shares. "Why not?" shrugged the owners of the rail line. "We're not going anywhere as we are. Maybe this fellow will build the corporate empire he talks about building. We won't be worse off."

Obtaining permission from state authorities to abandon unprofitable runs, Ronnie was able to dispense with half of his rolling stock. "Now," he told George as they drank coffee together one morning, "Rontronics has some cash as well as a lot of stock. I think I will call the board of directors into session and authorize issuance of some convertible securities, which we will, of course, register with the Securities and Exchange Commission. They can be used to buy our next acquisition. We have no earnings yet, although I expect to realize some now that the unprofitable rail runs are off our backs. The balance sheet looks better. It has some assets now."

That is the shell game. As played by the Ronnies and Georges of Wall Street the shell game calls for repetition of the acquisition-for-securities maneuver. This is a play you cannot do without having good legal and accounting brains on your side. The regulatory authorities must be considered. And you have to sell managements of target companies on desirability of merger. "But shucks," Ronnie confided. "That isn't costly. They are convinced that Rontronics is going to be something big one day—so am I—and want to ride along for a piece of the action in the form of stock. They are also issued warrants. If things go well, the warrants will make them rich."

Sometimes, a company is acquired with its own cash. Securing interested backers, promotional merger operators have arranged acquisition of blocks of stock using borrowed funds, then repaid the loans, after acquisition, from cash in the treasury of a target company.

The shell game, the buy-for-stock play, and the gambit of buying a corporation with its own money, may seem something Horatio Alger would have looked on with distaste. The truth is that Horatio's heroes weren't smart enough. There is nothing nonlegitimate about these things, provided they are done with circumspection. They are in no way legally or morally wrong.

"Have you seen the Special Drawing Rights which the International Monetary Fund is sponsoring?" a broker in the merger-acquisition field asked me. "People call them 'paper gold.' That is just what they are—paper. Yet no one terms the SDRs 'funny money.' They are not different from the 'money' with which corporate mergers are cemented."

Just how far and how fast you can go with mergers is illustrated by the case of Al Lapin, whom we met in the preceding chapter as he built the fast-food chain from a beginning with partly borrowed dollars. The July 23, 1969, issue of the Merrill Lynch, Pierce, Fenner and Smith publication, *Investors Reader*, further reported:

> In 1966 INT bought franchisor United Rent-All, the oldest and largest chain of rental equipment stores in the US. There are now over 400 outlets which rent party supplies, medical equipment, tools, sporting goods. The three years since have seen 13 more acquisitions. . . . Revenues grew from $626,000 in fiscal 1959 to $38,800,000 in the August 1968 year. Profits in the same period multiplied a hundred fold to $4,190,000.

One of the largest conglomerate corporations in the United States is Gulf and Western Industries, Inc., with sales in 1968 of $1.5 billion. It grew to that size from a small auto parts firm, purchased as nucleus for the future empire by Charles Bluhdorn.

If you, George, or Ronnie are going to duplicate a feat like that, you have to know the step-by-step rules:

A Merger Pro Can Help Anyone who starts a professional football team is not likely to find Joe Namath or Bart Starr immediately available. He will be well advised, nevertheless, to obtain experienced pro talent and not rely upon players, however eager and promising, whose range of expertise is hardly broader than his own.

It likewise helps to have a pro at your side when you are planning to travel the merger route. Happily, there are many of these professionals. When you first begin they may not care to play on your small team. As soon as you reach minimum size, it can be a good idea to put one in charge of your operation.

"These people can do for you much the same things that a marriage broker did for boys and girls in lands where this kind of matchmaking was traditional," says a practitioner of the art. "He brings together people who are likely to make happy marriages."

One such merger-marriage broker maintains a computer file of prospects, matching needs and personalities of people involved. Another goes in for what he termed "creative matchmaking," generally involving an effort to match the needs of one company with the capacities of another in the same way a new salesman is instructed to ask his customer the creative question, "And how about some of the season's new neckties to go with your shirt, sir?" A sound description was offered by one firm: "We serve as buffers between buyers of companies and sellers of companies."

Many of these firms specialize in finding smaller, family-type outfits for the merger-minded Ronnie or George seeking diversification and growth.

You Will Have To Be Aware of What Makes a Good Acquisition
Arithmetic worked up on one potential deal illustrates this:

The company was in the transportation field. It made only tiny profits, but possessed stock in another transportation company. The latter stock was listed on the New York Stock Exchange. In addition, the treasury held idle capital. The stock of our target company traded at around 16 over the counter.

"Now if we can obtain controlling interest by driving it up no higher than 22, or possibly by making a tender offer around 20 to 21, we might achieve a lot," my partner pointed out. "Here's the way I figure. We would receive, first, the complete transportation network, not a very profitable one and not easy to evaluate, but—

"We would receive enough in marketable stock to make about $17 per share. Say we got that and then sold it off. We could pay out the proceeds to stockholders as a special nonrecurring dividend. We would then have a net cost per share of about $5. And that isn't all.

"In the treasury, according to the latest company report, are cash and equivalents which, if my desk calculator is doing its work faithfully, are worth about $4 per share. We would have that, too.

"Then we might pay out the cash to stockholders, as we consider doing with proceeds from the stock sale, and leave ourselves with a cost of only about a dollar per share for which we would be possessors of a complete transportation network, the rights to operate, and the equipment. Then on the adjusted cost the return, instead of being tiny, would become big.

"Or we could pay out half of the cash and equivalent in the treasury and retain the rest to refurbish equipment and try to make this dowdy old transportation thing into something really big. It might, in turn, become the nucleus of a fresh conglomerate if we are able to pep up the profits."

That is interesting arithmetic. The most interesting thing is that such figures can be worked up by you on a number of companies. But they do not always and inevitably lead to wealth. In our case, the project was abandoned because further research developed the fact that around 50 percent of outstanding stock was in the hands of a few management men who were not willing to sell. Rather than buck odds of a fight with entrenched management, probably assisted by some of the older stockholders, the campaign was reluctantly tabled.

As a sidelight to this true story—circumstances which might make the company recognizable have been changed—the arithmetic proved so compelling that years later another group with strong conglomerate backing did succeed in overthrowing the "in" group and took over our target company.

A target company for acquisition purposes should be one which represents, in your hands if not in the hands of current owners, greater value than the price which must be paid out to get it. That value might be in cash or things like stock which can be turned into cash. It might be in the form of unrealized potential. The value might consist of needed entry into a new field at a cost less than trying to break into it cold. There are many reasons why a merger can make logical sense.

Eugene S. Merrill, vice-president of Stone and Webster Management Consultants, Inc., has this to say on the subject of appraising comparative values of acquiring and acquired companies:

> . . . a full-fledged study should be made using all the financial factors and techniques needed to evaluate stocks which are not traded and for which no market appraisal is available. However, even for mergers and acquisitions involving companies with listed stocks that are actively traded, it is usually advisable to make the same thorough study and analysis. *It must always be remembered that the accepted exchange ratio freezes the value relationship permanently.* An acquisition that eventually results in a dilution of earnings per share will not be welcome to the stockholder merely because it was based on actual market price as of the date of merger.

Mr. Merrill's firm has suggested the following checklist for judging attraction of a prospective acquisition:

Financial:
   √ Restatement of financial statements on comparable basis.
   √ Depreciation analyses.
   √ Operating and financial forecasts.
   √ Cash flow analyses.
   √ Effects on return, cash flow, earnings per share.
   √ Results under alternative methods of acquisition.
Tax:
   √ Tax effects of acquisition route chosen.
   √ Effects of tax items to be inherited if merger route chosen, i.e., loss carryovers, earnings and profits, accounting methods, depreciation methods, adjusted tax cost of assets, etc.

✓Effect of assets to be acquired on composite tax depreciation rates, depreciation reserves, and reserve ratios under
"guide line" rules.

Valuation:

✓Independent appraisal of assets to be acquired if needed
for apportionment to elements recoverable for tax purposes.

✓Independent valuation of enterprise to be acquired as protection in the event of subsequent minority stockholder
suits.

Operational:

✓Management and staff reorientation.

✓Personnel absorption and meshing of rates of pay, union
jurisdiction, fringe benefits, etc.

✓Public relations, announcements to maximize the benefits.

✓Realignment of sales and promotional programs.

✓Effect on production, distribution and warehousing facilities.

Know the Tactics of Merger   The happiest mergers, like the
happiest marriages, are made by mutual consent. But occasionally, mergers come about only after bitter battle, sometimes
after one side has been battered into bloody submission. As a
way of making happy marriages between persons, this method
has little to commend it. But in the rough-and-tumble world
of mergers and acquisitions the result is often successful.

The old-fashioned courtship is exemplified by the negotia-
tions of Ronnie and George in arranging their acquisitions.
The principals sit down. They talk. If they agree that the two
parts together will do better than either alone, bring about
the synergism which conglomerate managers like to cite, then
the merger proceeds amicably and swiftly. It is a course recommended for the beginning merger master who wants to start a
corporate empire from scratch.

As his empire gets older and farther from the scratch point,
however, he will sometimes encounter situations too complicated to be settled by quiet discussion. Bigger mergers involve publicly traded stock. They usually start with the ac-

quiring company's establishing a position through purchase in the open market. Long ago, the next thing to do was to declare proxy war and line up for a pitched battle which, more times than not, left both parties losers. Better tactics have been evolved since that simple shoot-it-out day.

Now an acquirer with a marriage gleam in his eye is likely to make a tender offer. He picks a figure comfortably above the going market price for the stock of the company he wants to acquire and makes an offer for the stock. It may be in cash. More often it is a package of securities, perhaps common mixed with convertibles or warrants, perhaps securities with a salting of cash. The idea is to make the package worth enough to get people to tender stock, but not so high that the acquiring company acquires a turkey instead of a bargain.

In making up a package, the merger master is usually careful to avoid dilution of his own earnings. Hence the frequent inclusion of convertibles and warrants with conversion prices sufficiently above the going market price of the common to bring about a probability that conversion will be made in an orderly way over a lengthy time rather than all at once.

Usually, the tender offer involves a deadline by which stock must be put in the hands of an escrow agent and a provision that the company making the offer reserves a right to refuse all tenders unless a minimum amount of stock is offered.

Learn about the Wondrous World of Merger Accounting   "My earnings," the president of one merger-minded company is reported to have said loftily when a reporter questioned the validity of certain figures on his annual statement, "are whatever I say they are." He was telling the truth. In the wonderful world of merger-acquisition accounting, things are not as simple as they might seem to a businessman who believes two and two must always equal four. Sometimes they equal six, even seven, and occasionally ten.

Nonaccountants are often shocked to discover that there is

no accepted way to keep books. In a field where two giant corporations compete, the first of these consolidates earnings of
its foreign subsidiaries. The second takes into profit consideration only the dividends actually paid into it from overseas. "If
Company A kept books as does Company B," a CPA said, "it
would have run deficits, not profits, for the last ten years, and
no one would regard it as a growth company. If company B
kept books the way Company A does, its earnings per share
would triple."

Whether to consolidate earnings of foreign subsidiaries or
count only dividends received is just one of dozens of options
a corporation faces. When a certified public accountant says in
the annual statement that his client company's books seem to
be kept in a normal sort of fashion, this means that the methods are unobjectionable from an accounting viewpoint and
consistent from year to year. That's all.

These wide choices offer acquirers of companies the opportunity to juggle methods without doing anything which in the
eyes of the law would be illegal. Sometimes simple bookkeeping viewpoints change a losing proposition into an almost immediate profit-maker without adding a dollar to sales or
subtracting a dollar from costs. You can only do something
like this once, of course. That is why some—not all by any
means—of the conglomerate companies keep on merging year
after year.

Moreover, the possessor of a corporation with a high price-
earnings ratio has a gimmick for increasing earnings whenever
he acquires or merges with a corporation having a low, pedestrian ratio. Go back to Moon Land Sales, mentioned in Chapter One. It would be fitting for such an exotic corporation to
sell at a high PER. Maybe 35. So its president, viewing his
thus far skimpy sales, might decide to make an offer for Downtoearth Doughnuts, selling for the same price of 40, but with
earnings of $4, to give it a price to earnings multiple of 10.
The merger goes through on a share-for-share basis. Down-

toearth Doughnuts becomes a division of Moon Land Sales.

Suddenly, Moon Land looks more impressive because its sales, hitherto only about $50,000 a year because the idea of a second home in space had not caught on as yet, has sales of $3 million. Only $50,000 comes from sales of moon surface, but the company size is more impressive than it had been. And—

Now the earnings of Moon Land are growing. The capitalization has doubled by shares issued for Downtoearth Doughnuts. But the profits have increased many times. So the vital earnings-per-share data so dear to financial analysts' hearts have gone up impressively. A few more analysts begin to recommend that investors buy Moon Land. After months, it is back selling for thirty-five times the new earnings which accrued after acquisition of Downtoearth Doughnuts. That makes a capital gain for Moon Land's owners, who are now ready to take on bigger and better acquisitions.

The above, of course, is a simplified explanation of some of the accounting options available to acquiring companies. The accounting profession is beginning to stir itself, some of its members aghast at the nonscientific state of its semiscience. Yet acquisition options remain. If you are going to pursue the merger Road to Wealth, you should be aware of them.

TO RECAP:

1. To obtain the "money" with which mergers are arranged and consummated, most merger-minded entrepreneurs begin by going public, incorporating if they are not already incorporated, and then selling shares to outside investors.

2. Another path leading into the merger road is to buy a "shell company" whose assets have been sold, leaving only the corporate shell.

3. Once possessed of a traded, negotiable, semiliquid stock,

the entrepreneur with mergers in mind uses these to purchase companies.

4. Sometimes, purchase of a company can be made using its own accumulated cash.

5. The merger movement is not confined to big operators. Some now-sizable national corporations have been built from very small beginnings by employing the colossal leverage of merger and acquisition.

6. Merger empires have been built within a single industry. But other, often bigger, empires are based upon gobbling up all kinds of unrelated corporations and relying on the economics of size, plus good top management, to make them better as parts of a whole than they were as separate, scattered entities.

7. Services of a merger broker can often help. He is a professional adept at finding potential mergers and bringing them to fruition. He is more likely to prove useful once an empire has been built up, however, than in its struggling days, since few of these experts serve for small fees.

8. A merger planner must be aware of the tactical steps likely to prove successful.

9. He must also be aware of the intricacies and possibilities of merger-acquisition accounting.

11
Seven Ways to Raise Capital

LEVERAGE! In past chapters we have seen how it can be applied to stocks, bonds, mutual funds, raw land, the remodel-and-resell real estate market, apartments and other big real estate, commodities, franchising, and the merger-acquisition game. In each instance, leverage can multiply the power of a very little bit of starting capital.

Provided you have the capital.

This chapter will tell you how you can get it, and after you have achieved the small starting monetary muscle power necessary to make the leverage plays work, how you can go after still greater sums of money. Although few of us are aware of it, nearly every family which is not reduced to complete destitution can lay its hands on starting capital. It can do so without impairing its standard of living, scrimping, eating peanut butter sandwiches instead of filet mignon, or robbing the nearest branch of the Consolidated Gotwads National Bank and Trust Co.

Many businessmen like to paint a "friendly" picture of themselves. You are advised to see your friendly jeweler, call upon the friendly plumber in the next block when your water heater breaks down, send dirty clothes to the friendly coin-op laundry, or contract with the friendly housewrecker if you want to make a parking lot out of the family homestead. To raise capital for leverage you might talk to some (or even all) of seven friendly fellows. To wit:

The Friendly Banker Man

Although he sits at a neat desk, usually within an imposing, sometimes marble-walled building, the banker is just as much a merchant with something to sell as the department store owner or car dealer. He employs a different sales tactic. He lets *you* ostensibly sell *him*. But he is a merchant all the same.

Keep that in mind when you go to a bank to talk about a loan. The officer with whom you talk business is anxious to say yes. And like other merchants, he wants to build an enduring relationship with clients like you, George, and Ronnie who give promise of growing into bigger clients over the years.

From your point of view, such an enduring relationship can be a good thing. When money gets tight, as it did in 1969, and before that in 1966, and as it probably will again from time to time, friendly bankers tend to remember which have been the friendliest of their clients when they sit down to apportion scarce loans. There are a hundred ways in which good bank relationships can make things go smoothly for an entrepreneur planning to travel the Roads to Wealth.

In a study published by the Small Business Administration, *Building Strong Relations with Your Bank,* James A. Cashin,

Chairman of the Department of Accounting and Finance of Hofstra University, wrote:

> It is important from the start, that you work to establish good relations before you need to borrow money. When you need money to finance inventory, for example, you should not be under pressure when you go to negotiate for it. An important key to building a strong relationship with the bank: develop a personal contact with an officer or other responsible employee in the bank. Six steps can be helpful: (1) show good faith, (2) give the bank volume, (3) provide the bank with financial data, (4) invite the banker to visit your place of business, (5) introduce the banker to your top assistant, and (6) discuss future plans with your banker.

But your bank won't lend on faith, trust, or friendship. It will want collateral. It will also need to know the purposes for which the loan might be used, a projection of expected profit, and the current business facts about you.

If you already own stocks, bonds, or other securities, these make the best kind of collateral. A loan can be arranged in moments, and in most cases a banker will give a better break on interest than he will on less-liquid collateral.

How much he will lend depends upon the purpose for which you borrow. Should you borrow to buy other securities, he is compelled to lend only whatever margin the Federal Reserve System allows brokers to advance. When you use securities for collateral in order to raise funds for noninvestment purposes, he might lend as much as 75 percent or 80 percent of the immediate value of stocks and, depending upon the quality, up to 90 percent on bonds. Mutual fund collateral rates the same as stocks since you are borrowing on equity in the fund's portfolio.

If you are an old client and he knows you well, or if your reputation in the community is topnotch, the friendly banker may, in excess of amity, lend on your signature alone. But he is not likely to lend a large amount. Nor will he give you the best possible interest rate, since he is taking more of a risk than if he were to lend on a package of stocks and bonds which he could, at need, sell quickly and at low commission to cover a defaulted loan.

When your signature alone won't get the amount you want, it is frequently possible to borrow with cosigners or guarantors. But you're still down in the low amount brackets with this method. Moreover it is not easy to ask a friend to put his future welfare on the line by backing your word.

The fellow behind the banker's desk will also make loans against leases (say you own a two-apartment dwelling and rent out half of it; you can sometimes assign the uncollected portion of the lease as collateral); on real estate; warehouse receipts, if you're in a business where this applies; on chattel mortgage covering such items as store and office equipment or vehicles (this isn't the best kind of collateral and should be used only if other ways of raising funds fail); on accounts receivable (money owed to you by your customers, patients or, clients); a savings account (sometimes people prefer to borrow on their own savings passbooks rather than drain these down to nothing); the cash surrender value of life insurance.

At times of high interest rates you will be wise to avoid a lengthy loan. Why pay 8 to 10 percent for a loan now and have it extend five years into the future, when the probabilities are that, if money conditions follow historical cycles, you may later be able to get similar loans at half the interest costs? Some people borrow for relatively short periods of time, retaining an option to renew on the same terms. Others write into the agreement a clause allowing them to pay the loan in full before it matures should funds no longer be needed or if they can be replaced at lower interest cost.

Before you sign a note, you should understand that interest charges fall into two classifications. Which of these your note specifies will govern the cost of your borrowing. Some of these differences were discussed in Chapter Five in reference to mortgage loans.

Applying what he termed "simple interest" and "add-on interest" to bank loans, Robert C. Gremley, manager of the Commercial Loan Department of the State National Bank of Evanston, Illinois, and a lecturer in the Graduate Division of the American Institute of Banking, wrote in the August, 1969, issue of *Dental Economics:*

> The subject of interest rates is often misunderstood because of the way it is explained by the financial institutions. . . . The two basic methods in use today are "simple interest" and "add-on (or discount) interest". . . . In almost all cases you will be paying more money for the borrowed funds when the interest rate is computed on an "add-on" rate.

The accompanying table * shows how a loan of $10,000 at 7 percent interest changes to about 13.5 percent if computed at "add-on" rates.

Haggle to get the lowest interest rate you can. This will be measured by comparison with "prime rate," the percentage (set generally by New York banks and followed by banks elsewhere in the country) which is charged to the best customers and lowest risks. American Can is a prime risk; the likelihood of its defaulting on a loan is too small to consider. Joe's Cannery down the block is not a prime risk. But Joe will bargain for a loan by asking his banker: "How much above prime will you charge me?" The answer may range from one-quarter of 1 percent to 1½ percent above prime. Which you will get depends upon how good a customer Mr. Friendly Banker considers you, the kind of collateral you offer, the risks he believes inherent in your loan, and possibly upon whether he enjoyed his lunch an hour ago. The figure he quotes does not have to be a final one. It is subject to negotiation.

After you settle interest rate, watch out for two words. These are "compensating" and "balance." We met this devastating gimmick earlier in Chapter Three. Banks frequently de-

* Courtesy Robert C. Gremley and *Dental Economics* magazine.

SIMPLE INTEREST

Borrowed Funds: $10,000
Rate: 7 percent   Term: 5 years (60 months)

	Principal	Interest
1st year	$ 2,000	$ 645.10
2nd year	2,000	520.00
3rd year	2,000	385.80
4th year	2,000	241.80
5th year	2,000	87.40
Total	$10,000	$1,880.10

Monthly payment $198.10

ADD-ON INTEREST

Borrowed funds: $10,000
Rate: 7 percent   Term: 5 years (60 months)

	Principal	Interest
1st year	$ 2,000	$ 700
2d year	2,000	700
3d year	2,000	700
4th year	2,000	700
5th year	2,000	700
Total	$10,000	$3,500

Monthly payment $225

mand that borrowers maintain compensating balances on loans. It works this way: Suppose George and Ronnie borrow $50,000. The banker asks 20 percent compensating balance. That means that George and Ronnie must maintain a minimum balance of $10,000 in their account at all times. The bank has lent them the money but then denied them the use of a portion of it so that the bank's deposit figures will be bigger. However, George and Ronnie must pay interest on $50,000. Thus the true interest is higher than quoted and the useful part of the loan less than signed for.

There are times when you won't be able to haggle your way out of the compensating balance trap or find another friendly banker in the next block who won't also demand a pound of financial flesh in the form of minimum balance.

In such a spot, you can turn to special lenders. Their advertisements are to be found on financial pages of major papers each day. Typically, they stand willing to transfer enough deposits they own to your bank to furnish the compensating balance you are required to have in your account. Thus the balance of the borrowing is freed for leverage uses. The special finance firm collects a charge for its service which, it is true, will add to the overall cost you incurred to rent that $50,000, but which will make it possible for you to use the full amount.

Sometimes loans are hard to get under any conditions. The friendly banker shakes his head sadly and says, "I would like to help, George. But I just can't do it. You haven't enough collateral or don't meet other minimum requirements." If he is a knowledgeable as well as a friendly banker, he may next suggest that you talk to the Small Business Administration.

The SBA's definitions of "small" are not constricting. If you employ more than 250 people, you aren't small. You have to have "independent" company ownership. This rules out subsidiaries of big corporations. If SBA approves the purposes for which you want to borrow, it can lend 80 percent of your needs. The Small Business Administration may arrange to have part of this carried by the friendly bank which turned you down in the first place but which is generally willing to go along once government guarantee has been thrown in to sweeten the pot.

The Friendly Insurance Man

He is not necessarily the man who sells and services your insurance policies. He is more likely a friendly fellow hidden deep in the insurance company's back offices. He becomes popular with borrowers at times when money is tight and expensive because of a clause written into many policies.

This clause provides that the policyholder can borrow against cash surrender value accumulated in his policy, paying 5 to 6 percent interest. In 1969, with the biggest and primest borrowers paying 8 percent, loans like that looked like easy money.

An insurance company loan is usually used for initial capital, sometimes the seed money required to swing a bigger loan. But all insurance loans are not small. There were reports in 1969 of companies which borrowed against cash surrender values of all the big ticket policies carried on executives and, on occasion, obtained money approaching $1 million at a rate that might have made other borrowers green with envy.

The Friendly Mortgage Man

Some pointers to have in mind before negotiating a mortgage were considered in Chapter Five. There, we looked at the mortgage as a lending method applied to raw land. It is also applicable to mortgaging apartments, homes, etc., when these are chosen as Roads to Wealth.

When you are in need of initial funds, the first thing to consider is—what will you mortgage?

Your home? This might seem dangerous, but it is a legitimate thing to use when you require starting capital. Mortgage it only if existing sources of income make you certain that you will be able to repay.

Mortgage on land or buildings used for a principal profession or business are also legitimate collateral. But the same consideration applies. Do this only if reasonably sure you can repay.

If these things are already covered with mortgage paper, you can seek a second mortgage. It will cost more to get this, and you will not be able to obtain long-term money as with a first obligation on the property. But considerable sums can frequently be raised in short time on second mortgages.

In the present money atmosphere (this is written in the fall of 1969), interest rates are as high as ever in history. Which should make you wonder—will you do better waiting for mortgage rates to come down again? They *will* come down eventually, but probably not soon. Many people whose field of study is money believe that just as we had an era of unprecedented cheap money in the forties and fifties, we may now be in the beginning of an age of tighter, more expensive money. "It is something corporate planners are learning to live with," one consultant told me. "There is no reason anyone else should consider himself exempt. Money may get easier than it is now after a time. But we won't go back to those halcyon, easy, cheap interest days of a decade and more ago. These, remember, were abnormal in the light of historical precedent."

Rates will eventually come down. But will costs go up even more? That is something you must consider in the light of local conditions. The answer has to be a personal one, tailored to your needs and your long-term plans.

The Friendly Leasing Man

Leasors are not in the market for buying and renting homes. But they might be interested in a sale-leaseback on your business land. Sale-leaseback means that you sell the land and store building of the George's Clam Juice Steak House to the lessor. You take back at the same time a long-term lease to the place. Arrangements can sometimes be made on land already under mortgage. In doing this you will have freed the capital tied up in mud, concrete, bricks, and mortar. One sale-leaseback specialist, Richard E. Patzer, Director of Sales for Nationwide Development Co., points out the diversity of activities in his field:

Our present complex contains over 40 leased properties, including offices, warehouses, financial institutions, department stores, supermarkets, convenience food stores, truck terminals and drive-in restaurants. We also lease land on which two medical-professional buildings are located. . . . We prefer a basic lease term of at least twenty years. If a buy-back option is desired, we will consider including one, usually to be exercised only after the tenth year and at a pre-established figure, usually not less than the amount of the original investment, feeling land appreciation offsets building depreciation.

Conventional leasing setups are applied to automobiles (you can free the capital you might spend to buy a new personal car by renting one instead) and trucks; all kinds of equipment; big things, such as the interior furnishings of motels and office buildings; or little things, such as TV sets. Seagoing ships have been leased. You can even rent people through the temporary help agencies.

Leasing is no cure-all, and both advantages and drawbacks should be taken into account. On the plus side of leasing are these points:

- There is a tax gimmick.

Often when you own something, you have to depreciate it for tax purposes on a lengthy table so that the cost is recovered only slowly. Much bookkeeping has to be done to obtain a tax saving which is occasionally minuscule. If inflation proceeds at the same pace as in recent years, moreover, the tax saving becomes one of decreasingly valuable dollars as the depreciation table stretches into the future. But leasing expenses do not have to be depreciated, stretched out, held to future years, or back-charged to years which have gone by. Generally, every cent put out for rent becomes a deduction in the year when it is expended.

- Maintenance is decreased, sometimes eliminated.

I discussed this question with an official of one leasing company. "We rent things either with or without maintenance contracts," he told me. "If you have a maintenance contract, we do everything. It is our piece of equipment and we keep it in shape for you. No fuss, muss, wear, tear, or bother. No maintenance crew. In effect, the lessee rents our maintenance crews when he rents an item with maintenance contract." (It is well to understand that not all maintenance contracts are as thoroughgoing as the one this man described. Some contracts call for upkeep only on certain kinds of breakdowns, leaving other repairs to the lessee.)

■ Consolidation of accounts is possible.

With equipment you own, cost is amortized on the books under a depreciation account. Repairs or routine service to the equipment go onto another account. When you pay taxes, a third entry is made. The salaries of men who keep equipment running go on a fourth account. One beauty of the leasing idea, according to many of its advocates, is that all these accounts and diverse entries are eliminated. Only rental must be entered. "It's the lessor's equipment, not mine," shrugged one owner. "In these days when it is so hard to get or keep good clerical help. I am delighted to get him to do the paperwork."

■ Early obsolescence need not be your worry.

Some equipment is made quickly obsolete—even antiquated —by advancing technology. If a sizable writeoff were to be made under those circumstances, profits might be penalized severely. "But when something gets out of date I call the leasing company, tell a man there, 'Hey, Harry, come get it and give us the later model'—then the obsolescence problem is his," reported one executive.

"Of course," he added, "all leasing contracts do not contain provision for this. If you want the obsolescence provision, as we do, you have to negotiate it into the contract—and usually pay extra for it."

■ Costs become fixed and predictable.

You own certain machines. For many years they require only routine services. Then they have a spate of breakdowns. You don't know on January 1 whether the twelve months ahead are going to be a mechanically smooth period or whether the equipment is going to obey Murphy's Law (which states that if a thing can go wrong it will) and fall to pieces with resulting multiple repairs and service. With equipment rented on service maintenance, your costs are fixed and known on January 1. It is the leasing contractor who has to worry whether Murphy's Law will be operative in the year ahead.

Those points look impressive. But they become worthwhile only if you decide that leasing is the best way to lay your hands on leverage capital for wealth building. Before you decide that the friendly leasing man has the answer, you should know some of the drawbacks of leasing:

■ At the end of the lease period you own nothing.

Reduce the leasing question to the small matter of an automobile. I investigated the cost of leasing versus buying a new model four-door automobile in the middle-price range. With trade-in of an average three-year-old car it could have been purchased, loaded with air conditioning, power steering, power brakes, and radio, for about $3,400. Added to purchase cost would be the recurring charges for lube jobs, oil changes, tire and battery replacement, and the other things routinely needed with a car. On a full maintenance contract, which furnished everything except gasoline, this same car could have been rented for about $160 monthly. For a two-year contract that came to $3,840, approximately the same amount as if the car had been purchased and maintenance costs assumed.

On a rental deal, the user of the car would possess nothing when his lease expired.

On a purchase deal he would still be owner of a two-year-old automobile.

Change "automobile" to almost any rentable item and you have the idea. Rentals are often designed to amortize building, equipment, etc., over the life of a lease.

■ The asset might increase rather than depreciate in real value.

This happens when prices of new equipment move up sharply or the equipment becomes hard to get. The older item may have a higher real present value than its cost. When items are rented, this occasional increase accrues to the lessor, not the lessee.

■ You lose the bookkeeping item of depreciation.

Depreciation in some instances can be as important as rental outgo in computing taxes. Your accountant or tax advisor should be consulted on this point before you assume that leasing always offers a saving. This is true particularly with real estate, where heavy early depreciation charges can turn ordinary income into eventual capital gains should a fully amortized building be sold when it no longer has depreciation usability.

■ A consolidated account sometimes costs more than many scattered small ones.

Sometimes packaged charges for services exceed what a firm might expect to pay if it were able to bargain for service with separate outside people.

The Friendly Institutional Fund Man

Institutions comprise mutual funds, pension trusts, banks' trust departments, insurance companies, and other vast conglomerations of capital. The then-chairman of the executive committee of the New York Stock Exchange, Gustave Levy, said in a speech in 1968 that approximately one-half of all nonmember trading on the Big Board was institutional. I have seen private projections that by 1975, 80 percent may be institutional.

Funds have proliferated in number while they have grown in size. They scramble, scratch, and fight among themselves to produce something called performance. The cry of the performer is: "Beat the market averages!" Of late, his goal has become one of beating the other fellow who is also out to beat the averages. Out of this competitive ding-dong emerges a financing opportunity for small entrepreneurs who want to grow into big commercial cats.

The go-go institutional managers increasingly use something called "letter stock." You can issue letter stock for the funds you need to leverage your way along the wealth roads. For example:

In the early growth years of George's Clam Juice Steak Houses, things became monetarily cramped. Extended as far as he could safely go, George needed a new infusion of capital to leverage the next leap forward. A friend suggested a talk with Fred Fundmanager, who was in charge of the common stock portfolio of a mutual fund.

Over lunch the following day, Fred explained the letter stock bit.

"Any new issue of stock generally has to be registered," he pointed out. "If you sell only within a state, you can probably go through the state securities authority. If you sell interstate, you must go through the U.S. Securities and Exchange Commission. Even with a shorter 'Regulation A' offering registration takes time, trouble, and legal expense. But if stock *isn't* publicly traded, that becomes a different thing.

"Your profit and loss statement and your balance sheet impress me. I believe you will probably go places if you get some more financing. Subject to a closer examination of George's Clam Juice Steak Houses, here is what we can do:

"Your book value—we have to use it in the absence of a value established by public markets—is about $9.00 for each share you now have outstanding. Taking George's on a twelve-times-earnings basis gives us a figure of $10.80 per share. Let's call it possible value of $10.00 per share. We will buy 50,000 shares at $8.00. To do it without the cost and time lags of registration, we give a letter of investment intent stating that the stock is bought for long-term investment and will not be thrown on the public market. Then you agree that at the end of two years, we will go through registration for this stock. You get your money now, no red tape, no waits. We get a bargain, bought at less than I figure the real value would be. Your costs to go through registration at this time might run as high as our discount. A deal?"

The Friendly Venture Capital Man

Don A. Christensen is president of Greater Washington Investors, Inc., a venture capital firm. (Although his firm is technology oriented, all venturers of capital are not restricted to the realm of the laser, integrated circuit, and far-out mathematics.) In an address to the Washington Society of Security Analysts on May 27, 1969, Mr. Christensen explained how venture investors do their thing:

> We are involved in the most exciting business that one could imagine—participating in the creation of what could be tomorrow's Polaroid or Xerox or Digital Equipment Corp. We call this "venture capital."
>
> I view venture capital as a melding together of the money and the experience within Greater Washington with the talents and creative energy of an outside management group to create a substantial enterprise. Basically, it is a dynamic and creative activity which brings together a number of factors to achieve an objective. Another way to describe our business is . . . a professional minority investor in technological growth enterprises. . . . We stand ready to assist our companies actively whenever they desire it, but do not manage them. Rather, we seek to invest only where a strong management—one of proven ability and integrity—already exists. . . . Together, there have been a total of 62 companies in the GWII portfolio. *A number of these were totally new ventures;* others, although young, possessed at least a limited operating history; and some were relatively mature companies into which earlier GWII portfolio companies had merged. In nearly every case we have worked closely with our portfolio company managements in meeting the inevitable corporate problems which a growing company faces. We have been through public offerings, mergers, acquisitions, reorganizations and liquidations.

There are scores of companies like Greater Washington. Some are big enough to be listed on the New York Stock Exchange. Others are regional or local. In some communities, venture capital companies have been formed as sidelines of banks or Small Business Investment Companies. Recently one such company advertised:

"ATTENTION GROWTH COMPANIES

"Long-term loans (5–20 years), equity capital and management counseling available. Funds in excess of $2 million to any one company. Working capital, expansions, acquisitions / mergers, entering new markets, refinancing, starting a new business."

The Friendly Underwriter Man

This is the man you see if you wish to go public as George did in the last chapter, where the mechanics of going public were discussed in simplified form. However, going public is not the thing every entrepreneur wants to do. In a recent advertisement, a leading investment banking firm pointed out drawbacks: "You'd do better to 'stay private,' " it noted

> . . . if you're not ready to disclose detailed financial information on a broad basis . . . if some of your shareholders want to realize cash for their holdings but the company and the rest of the shareholders want to remain privately owned . . . if you're reluctant at this time to dilute your equity interest . . . if sales and profits have temporarily suffered for non-recurring reasons . . . if an important labor contract or other significant development that may adversely affect earnings is hanging in the balance . . . if you feel that your middle management needs more time to develop before you are ready to assume the added responsibilities of public ownership . . . if the need for new money is of an urgency that makes it impossible to wait for the extended and uncertain period often required to fulfill the requirements for registration of a public offering . . . if the net income of your company is likely to increase substantially in the future, when a public offering can be effected on more advantageous terms.

Going public involves expense. That is why some companies prefer to issue letter stock, even at a discount. But face it. You are not going to get really big without eventually going public.

Most initial public offerings are small. A great number are made under SEC Regulation A. Several years ago, the Federal Reserve Bank of Boston commissioned a study of public financing of small corporations through Regulation A. Its findings are instructive today. The Bank's *New England Business Review* of October, 1966, reported:

> Although a few issuers had assets of over $1 million, most had considerably less. More than three-quarters had assets of less than half a million dollars; 37 percent had assets of less than $100,000. In terms of owners' equity, the figures were even lower with the median at $80,000.
>
> The typical offering was common stock with expected proceeds of about $250,000. Roughly one-third of the sampled issues were of the maximum $300,000 size. About 15 percent of the offerings were debt, preferred, and combination issues and these were from older, relatively large companies with more equity.
>
> In general the offerings were of sizeable proportions relative to the existing scale of operations, thus reflecting the importance of the issue for corporate expansion. Out of 78 sampled issues, 60 percent were successfully marketed either by promoters or underwriters, with success defined as the sale of at least 85 percent of the proposed dollar offering. Of the successful issues, more than one-half were completed within 2 months from the initial date of the offering. Although 10 issuers achieved success in 6 months or longer the probabilities of being so fortunate diminish as time passes. The study data suggest that the chances of floating successful issues would improve if those that were not selling rapidly were withdrawn after a few months and new offerings made at a later, more opportune time.

The study further suggests that if you are going public, you will do better to use an underwriter than to try selling stock on your own as a few small companies have tried to do.

"A factor related to successful marketing was found to be commercial underwriting," the survey noted.

> Underwriting agreements in the small issues market are almost always on a "best efforts" basis; that is, the underwriter agrees to do his best to sell the issue but, failing to do so, is not obligated to buy the unsold securities. Although this method offers no guarantee of success, more than twice as many commercially underwritten issues were successfully marketed as those offered directly by promoters or officers of the issuers. Furthermore, commercial underwriters sold on the average 90 percent of the amount of each issue initially offered while direct promoters succeeded in selling only 50 percent. . . . Because of their knowledge of the market and its requirements, the underwriters, in many cases, were in a position to advise the issuers they served on such helpful matters as pricing and promotion—which might increase the market's interest in the stock offered.

TO RECAP:

1. Seven main avenues are open for financing small businesses into big enterprises. These are bank borrowing, mortgages, leasing, insurance, new ventures financiers, issuance of letter stock, going public.

2. An enduring relationship with a single helpful bank can be worth cultivating.

3. Banks occasionally (and usually at higher interest cost) lend on a signature alone. But most loans must be based upon collateral. Decide in advance what collateral is best for you.

4. A lender will want to see a profit and loss statement if you are already in business. He will need to be told the purposes of the loan and to see a projection of expected profit from the project to which borrowed funds will be put.

5. Where possible, avoid certain kinds of borrower-lender arrangements. Stay away from compensating balances. In time of high interest rate beware a long-term loan that does not

have arrangement for renegotiating should money ease in the future. Be cautious when offered "add-on" interest instead of simple interest. Depending upon the length of the note, this might come to twice the amount that would be charged as straight interest and is sometimes three or four times simple interest charges.

6. Borrowers who seek business loans and cannot obtain them from normal banking and borrowing sources can line up Small Business Administration funds.

7. Many life insurance policies have provision for lending against cash surrender values at rates which seem tiny in tight money times. Such loans often provide low-cost sources for seed capital.

8. Mortgages on business land or buildings or on your home provide for longer-term borrowing. Second mortgages go at higher interest rates, but if the money brings in more than it costs, even this expensive source is worth investigation.

9. Leasing is the newest form of raising money. You can lease land, buildings, equipment, vehicles, even (through temporary help agencies) people to work for you. Leasing frees capital formerly tied up in fixed assets and allows it to be used as leverage for expansion and growth. Leasing frequently has tax advantages, too. But there are disadvantages as well as plus factors in leasing, and these should be examined carefully.

10. Issuance of "letter stock" is a far-out, little-understood way to raise equity money without going through the throes and expense of registering a securities issue. It involves agreement to register the "letter" securities at a later date.

11. Specialized companies invest in new ventures, extending capital and management assistance to growing companies. Usually, venture capital firms regard themselves as professional minority stockholders.

12. Going public is complicated and often expensive. But a venture which is to grow to great size must face this sooner or later. A study shows that help from a professional new-issues underwriter is likely to bring in more than it costs.

Index